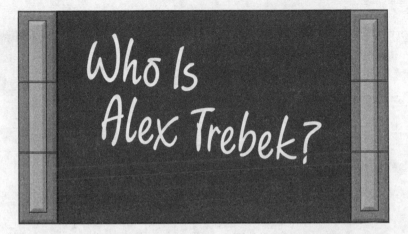

BELOVED
TV HOST

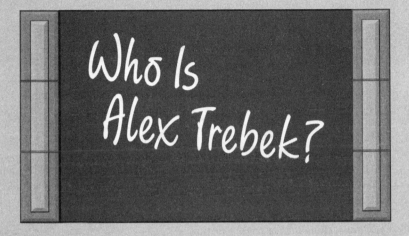

Who Is Alex Trebek?

A BIOGRAPHY

LISA ROGAK

ST. MARTIN'S
GRIFFIN
NEW YORK

For Alex . . . **My** *Alex*

The Library of Congress has cataloged the hardcover edition as follows:

Names: Rogak, Lisa, 1962- author.
Title: Who is Alex Trebek? : a biography / Lisa Rogak.
Description: First edition. | New York : Thomas Dunne Books, 2020. | Includes bibliographical references and index.
Identifiers: LCCN 2020011927 | ISBN 9781250773661 (hardcover) | ISBN 9781250773678 (ebook)
Subjects: LCSH: Trebek, Alex, 1940- | Television personalities—United States—Biography.
Classification: LCC PN1992.4.T6325 R64 2020 | DDC 791.4502/8092—dc23
LC record available at https://lccn.loc.gov/2020011927

ISBN 978-1-250-79814-5 (trade paperback)

Our books may be purchased in bulk for promotional, educational, or business use. Please contact your local bookseller or the Macmillan Corporate and Premium Sales Department at 1-800-221-7945, extension 5442, or by email at MacmillanSpecialMarkets@macmillan.com.

First St. Martin's Griffin Edition: 2021

10 9 8 7 6 5 4 3 2 1

CONTENTS

INTRODUCTION

The vast majority of Americans who have spent any amount of time watching *Jeopardy!*—even occasionally—would be forgiven for thinking that Alex Trebek has been around forever. He seems frozen in time, albeit in a calm, soothing manner, even when he frowns at a nervous contestant for missing an easy answer.

Because after hosting the iconic game show for more than thirty-five years, Alex has been part of the fabric of American culture for longer than many viewers have been alive.

"He just seems sort of immortal," the CNN legal analyst Jeffrey Toobin has said.

"I've been on the air for fifty years, so I'm like a member of the family," Alex said. "'Oh, there's Alex, we'd better get him a drink and get him some French fries or something.'"

That omnipresence remains true whether you're comfortably ensconced at home or cheering on tournament champions at your favorite watering hole. And if you're on the road in an unfamiliar city, his presence can be even more of a balm.

"When you arrive in a hotel room where you have no real sense of where you are, turning *Jeopardy!* on is always kind of a grounding experience," said Jonah Engel Bromwich, a domestic correspondent with *The New York Times.*

This grounding is true regardless of age. Indeed, YouTube videos abound, showing small children and babies crawling toward the TV and laughing as soon as the first notes of the *Jeopardy!* theme song start playing. Back in the mid-1980s, before she could walk, my niece Sara would giggle and bounce up and down in place whenever those iconic notes rang through the tinny TV speaker.

And while lesser-known celebrities might be offended by being tagged as "the world's greatest robot," Alex has always celebrated the moniker. "I'm the Energizer Bunny," he said. "I just keep on going."

However, few fans are aware that his penchant for predictability and longevity are largely the result of a childhood fraught with insecurity, which came in the form of his parents' separation and eventual divorce as well as getting packed off to a boarding school where he didn't know a soul. Scraping through college penniless, his basic expenses just barely covered by menial, boring jobs, didn't foster a strong sense of security, either.

So it's no wonder that when he got his first real job as an announcer with the CBC—the Canadian Broadcasting Corporation—he stayed for twelve years, which is an eternity in the entertainment world. For many, a long stint like that could have been horribly stifling, but for Alex it was anything but, since he hosted a stunningly diverse variety of shows—from curling to popular music—on both radio and

TV. It helped that he had a voracious appetite for learning new things.

"I'm curious about everything," he said, "even things that don't interest me."

So when *Jeopardy!* came along, it seemed to be a match made in heaven. "I love acquiring knowledge, even useless knowledge," he admitted.

Given his need for both security and variety, it's no wonder that *Jeopardy!* has suited him so well: it's been a long-term gig with a dizzying array of new facts and things to learn in every single show.

But it was a long, hard-fought road to get there.

Since *Jeopardy!* first went on the air in 1984, approximately four hundred other game shows have come and gone. "I've been lucky throughout my life," said Alex. "So many of the good things that have happened to me have happened by accident."

His curiosity has also led to a strong work ethic. "I don't ever turn down work," he said. "I learned a long time ago if someone offers you something, you accept it."

But this practice has had a definite downside over the years, as this self-described workaholic has regularly slid into a life of perfectionism and imbalance. "I am highly competitive, but more with myself than others, since I'm always trying to better myself," he said.

"I wish I could stop and smell the roses," he lamented.

Alex has never been your typical Hollywood icon, spilling out onto the red carpet at Hollywood premieres to see and be seen, or making the rounds of the morning talk shows to provide his ego with an easy boost. In fact, he's the antithesis of that, driving a half-ton Dodge Ram 1500 pickup to the studio most days, and loving nothing more than digging up a patch of lawn to pinpoint a busted water pipe and then rummaging around in his garage—which contains only tools; there's no room for a vehicle—for the exact two-and-a-quarter-inch pipe for the job.

During his entire tenure on *Jeopardy!* he's never once apologized for being a game-show host, though occasionally he's pointed out that the long-running program is a *quiz* show, not a game show. In fact, he's considered his field to be a particular point of pride. "I think game shows were the beginning and best of reality television," he said.

He's been particularly proud of the influence that the show has had on families. "We are the kind of program that you can watch with every member of your family," he said. "There's something for kids and grandparents—everyone can play. You can all spend a half hour together without feeling you have to flee the room to go watch your own show."

How many shows can you say *that* about? And while many celebrities look to their jobs to feed their self-esteem, Alex clearly has taken a different tack.

"My job has provided me with opportunities to explore the world geographically, socially, and philanthropically, and doing that has allowed me to develop as a human," he said.

But while he's been busy working on his intellect, Alex has readily admitted that his natural tendency to always be on guard against being hurt or abandoned again—accounting for his characteristic remoteness on the show—has meant that he's held back a little too much when it comes to his personal interactions with people. "It seems as if I have led my entire life as if I were considering a career in politics," he acknowledged. "I didn't want to make any mistakes."

However, that remoteness is in part what many viewers have latched onto for years, decades even, and is clearly something they crave. "Like many fathers, he has defined himself largely through emotional distance," said Sam Anderson, a staff writer with *The New York Times Magazine.* "This is part of his charm."

But happily, well into midlife, Alex finally learned to relax—when he met Jean Currivan, the woman who would become his wife, and when he became a father for the first time, at the age of fifty.

It's impossible to conceive of *Jeopardy!* without Alex Trebek, though of course his announcement in March 2019 that he had been diagnosed with stage IV pancreatic cancer has made his fans come face-to-face with that possibility sooner than they ever anticipated. "Greatest of All Time" champion Ken Jennings became visibly upset at the mere suggestion that he would make a good replacement as host.

"I can't imagine anybody but Alex," he said.

Alex, it seems, has made his peace with his fate, and any emotional and physical difficulties that he's faced have been softened somewhat by the outpouring of love, gratitude, and prayers he's received since making his illness public. "I had no idea that our show and myself had such an impact on the lives of so many people out there," he said with characteristic modesty.

But fans weren't surprised in the least. After all, when he was once asked what one word best described him, he answered, "It's '*solid*.' [The word] is that important to me; it says you're there to help other people if they need help, and to lend proper perspective in difficult situations."

And that's what millions of fans have always known and loved about Alex Trebek and what he represents—that he's solid, and pragmatic, and that despite his struggles, he's never lost sight of what really matters, a quality that all of us aspire to.

"Success is dependent on so many outside influences, but happiness comes from inside you," he said. "If you are centered properly, then you are at peace. And it doesn't matter whether you were trying to achieve this goal and you didn't reach it, because you enjoyed the journey, and found so many worthwhile things along the way."

1

PILOT, DOCTOR, OR PRIME MINISTER?

When Alex Trebek was twelve years old, he caught a glimpse of his future, only he didn't know it at the time.

In 1952, television hadn't yet made it to the small apartment that he shared with his parents and younger sister in the working-class town of Sudbury, Ontario. His father was a chef at a hotel in town, the Nickel Range, and couldn't afford such an extravagance on his wages.

Even though he was a bookworm and inhaled new facts as if they were oxygen, young Alex became absolutely transfixed the first time he encountered this brand-new technology that delivered not only audio like the radio, but pictures as well, just like the movies. His father had relatives across the border in Canton, Ohio, and in the summer of 1952, when Alex had just turned twelve, the Trebeks paid a visit there, only to find the entire family gathered around a big wooden box with glass on one side.

He settled in with his relatives to watch a Cleveland Indians baseball game. Though he could hardly see the players—the

picture was full of snow and the players were blurry blobs—
that didn't stop everyone from sitting in front of the set for
two hours, barely moving a muscle. "It was new," Alex said
decades later.

Up until then, he had relied upon radio for his access
to the world beyond. With just a Philco tabletop radio, he
listened for hours each night to drama, comedy, and game
shows from as far away as WBZ in Boston. And he never
missed the game show *You Bet Your Life* with Groucho Marx.
"I fell in love with Hollywood and show business [on the ra-
dio]," he said.

But with a TV, Alex loved that he didn't have to envision
the scene as he did when he listened to a ball game on the
radio; with television he could see it as well. It was almost as
good as going to a real game.

And just like the books that he loved, that small wooden
box opened up the world to him. He instinctively knew that
it would somehow help him to feed the insatiable curiosity he
had about absolutely everything in the world.

Alex was mesmerized. On the way back to Sudbury, he
couldn't stop thinking about it. Still, he knew better than to
badger his parents for a set of their own—money was tight,
as usual.

But what he didn't know is that that box would eventually
shape his career, and indeed his entire life.

It was a total accident that Alex Trebek's parents ever met.

When seventeen-year-old Lucille Lagacé met the tall,
dark stranger who showed up one day in her hometown of
Sudbury, Ontario—known as the Nickel Capital of the

World—in 1938, she took notice. She had always dreamed of seeing the rest of the world but didn't have the money or the inclination at a time when a girl's sole purpose was to find a husband and start a family. She wasn't opposed to that necessarily, but when the handsome man arrived on her doorstep, it didn't matter that he struggled with English, because she believed that with his arrival, the world had finally come to her.

George Edward Trebek was his name, and he had grown up in a small Ukrainian town near Kiev, where he'd had a rough childhood—his father had died shortly before his birth, and his mother passed away shortly afterward. An older sister took care of him, but he hung with a rough-and-tumble crowd of other orphaned kids and pretty much raised himself. While he was in his mid-teens, the Russian Revolution was suddenly looming, and in the social and economic chaos that followed, George decided the best thing to do was to leave the country, along with hundreds of thousands of other Russians. Canada was taking in immigrants to help fill jobs at factories and on farms, so he headed there.

Once George made it to Canada, he boarded a train bound for Winnipeg for a promised job on a farm. But when the train stopped in Sudbury, almost a thousand miles before his destination, he jumped off. It was unclear if he'd tired of the journey or if he'd gotten into a fight en route and the conductor had thrown him off the train. In any event, when Lucille saw him for the first time, she was enchanted, and after a whirlwind romance, they were married on December 16, 1939, in Sudbury. In the interim, George had found work as a chef in one of the restaurants in town, and they began their new life together.

Alex was born on July 22, 1940, and his sister, Barbara Ann, joined the family on October 14, 1941. The Trebeks lived in the Flour Mill section of the city, and though they didn't have much in the way of personal possessions to fill their small apartment, Alex would later recall that his father would give someone he had just met the shirt off his back. "My dad got along with everybody," said Alex.

In addition to having a wide circle of mostly Ukrainian friends, George was also quite fond of alcohol. "He'd sit and drink with people and chat with them forever," said Alex, who was seven years old when he started to hang out with his father and his friends. They liked to drink boilermakers, which traditionally is a shot of whiskey followed by a swig of beer. "But the Ukrainians got it backwards," Alex said years later. "They'd take a sip of beer and chase it down with a jigger of vodka. Those afternoon gatherings got to be pretty lively."

Lucille wasn't happy with her husband's fondness for booze and loud friends. She was quiet by nature, and enjoyed taking care of her family and home more than socializing. Plus, she didn't drink. But she also frequently became annoyed with George because he was all thumbs when it came to working on things around the house. She had grown up with brothers who were handy, and who all worked in the construction trade as carpenters and painters.

As a result, the tension between his parents would build to the point that they would argue. And though Alex didn't remember any physical fighting between his mother and father, when it came to her son, things could be different. "She was a disciplinarian," he said. "If I did something that she considered stupid, she would whack me pretty hard sometimes."

But so did most of his friends' parents back then, so he tried to take it in stride. And though he liked hanging out with his father and his friends, it was his mother he took after in the way he dreamed of exploring the world. Like Lucille, Alex was curious about everything, and he satisfied his thirst for knowledge by burying himself in books. "When I was a kid, I would read and get so excited I just couldn't wait to get to the next page," he said.

Besides the fact that he learned something new on every page, his voracious appetite for books could also distract him from his parents' fighting.

He even preferred the company of a book to spending time with friends his own age. "I was very bright but very shy, and the two combined to make a loner," he admitted.

Her son's preference for solitude and a good book concerned Lucille. "He kept very much to himself," she said decades later. "He'd sit on the steps and watch the other children play."

But Alex didn't mind. There was one book in particular that made a lasting impression on him. "I read *The Moonstone* by Wilkie Collins when I was about twelve and just couldn't devour the pages fast enough," he said of the classic story that T. S. Eliot considered the first and greatest of English detective novels. "I was entranced by this mystery novel, and it might be what inspired my love of reading," Alex said.

As much as he loved to read, Alex was also fascinated by

geography. Young Alex spent hours ogling maps, particularly of Africa. "It had the most countries and was mysterious," he said. "Asia was exotic, but Africa had the animals, the pygmies, the cannibals! It had everything a young boy would be fascinated in."

In addition to poring over maps, he read geography books and atlases that he checked out from the library, as well as copies of *National Geographic* magazine. Because money was tight, the Trebek family rarely subscribed to the monthly publication, but Alex knew there was one place he could count on seeing it. "I made it a point to go to a lot of doctor and dentist appointments," he said.

Between books and maps, he knew there was a big world out there, and he wanted to learn about all of it.

In addition to drinking and hanging out with his friends, George also liked to gamble and bet on the ponies. He'd frequently take Alex along on a streetcar to spend the afternoon at the horse track.

And young Alex loved the fact that his family observed two Christmases: one on December 25, and the Russian Orthodox holiday on January 7. He especially looked forward to the traditional French-Canadian meat pie known as *tourtière* that was served when they returned home from Christmas Eve midnight mass.

But *tourtière* was about as exotic as family dinners got. Even though George was a professional chef, it was Lucille who cooked for the family, and she mostly stuck to the standard meat-and-potatoes fare that was common in Northern Ontario.

Alex liked to hang out with his uncles as they worked on their houses and helped their sister with hers. He was fascinated by their skill at framing walls, installing windows, and painting hard-to-reach roof eaves, and they often gave him a small task he could perform alongside them.

He went to St. Louis de Gonzague, a Catholic school in the neighborhood, where he occasionally got in trouble. "I got whacked by the nuns for throwing snowballs and bothering the girls," he said. He hung out with a group of boys, and his best friend was the son of the owner of the hotel where George worked as a chef. The two of them liked to head to the outskirts of town to watch trucks from the mining companies pour molten slag—what was left after the nickel and other minerals were extracted from the ore—down the mountain; it looked like the hills were on fire, and the two boys loved it. "We couldn't imagine anything more fantastic," Alex said.

Overall, he was a good student. "My parents always said to me, 'Alex, get a good education and you can be anything you want to be,'" an adage he kept at the forefront of his mind. He also started to think about what he wanted to be when he grew up. The books he read were giving him lots of ideas, and one day, when he was about twelve, he wrote down the careers he'd like to pursue—*a pilot, a doctor, or prime minister of Canada*—and tucked the note away.

But then one winter everything changed, almost overnight. Alex was watching his sister and some of her friends playing on a frozen creek near their home. Alex thought it didn't look solid enough to walk on, so he told his sister to get onto the bank and he'd test it himself. As he suspected, parts of the creek were just a thin film of ice, and as he tested one spot, he fell through to the water below.

The other children started screaming, and adults raced over and pulled young Alex from the frigid water. That day, he learned that life could be taken away in an instant.

He doubled down on his resolve to learn everything he could while he was still able.

Alex's father was a pack rat. Growing up in extreme poverty in Ukraine, he had learned to hold on to everything he could because (a) he never knew when he'd find another like it, and (b) he figured he'd probably discover a use for it at some point.

Just as Alex was a good student in the classroom, he was also a quick study at home. "I've never thrown anything away," he admitted years later. Books were expensive, and though he borrowed them from the library, he loved them so much that he started to save up to buy one of his own, and he knew it had to be special.

The first book he ever purchased was a leather-bound edition of *Wuthering Heights;* he paid two bucks for it. He loved the way it felt—the heft of the book, its smooth leather— not to mention the fact that it was *his.* He was hooked, and he wanted more. For that, he needed money. So his father pulled some strings at the Nickel Range Hotel and got Alex a job as a bellhop after school and on weekends. Most tips were around ten cents, though a big spender would occasionally tip as much as a quarter. He was in the ninth grade at Sudbury High and figured he could juggle classes, homework, and a part-time job.

The week before Alex started his job, he traveled with his

class on a school trip to Montreal, Quebec City, and Ottawa. He arrived back in Sudbury late the night before he had to report for his first day of work the next morning, but he overslept and didn't wake up until his father called around noon to ask where he was. "It was a great way to start my career," said Alex.

But that was the least of his troubles. The fights between his parents had continued to escalate, and Lucille had finally had enough. One day she packed her bags and moved out, leaving the kids with George, since she couldn't afford to support them on the only type of menial job she was qualified for.

Alex was devastated. George and the kids moved from the apartment into a small suite at the Nickel Range. The stress of the separation was hard on Alex, and his grades started to slip. He buried himself in his books and listened to the radio to quell the loss as best he could, but seeing his family broken up had destroyed him. Meanwhile, his father soon realized that working a full-time job, trying to manage his anger and grief, and dealing with two traumatized children was too much for him. So he sent both kids off to boarding school, Alex heading to the prep school at the University of Ottawa, which was under the auspices of the Catholic Church.

The school was well regarded, with two hundred fifty boarders, two hundred day students, and forty-five priests living in the dormitory with the students. But the change of scenery didn't quell Alex's anger; if anything, it only fanned the flames. "I was one of the more difficult students in class," he admitted.

Though he managed to get along with most of the priests,

Alex felt that one of them—the prefect of discipline—had it in for him from the beginning. "He was narrow-minded and petty and he tried to make me miserable," he said, "and I was determined to do the same [to him]."

His attacks on the priest tended to take a passive-aggressive route. One day Alex saw a key ring sitting on a table, which he knew belonged to his nemesis. So he grabbed the keys and spent several hours unlocking every door in the building. He eventually handed in the keys, but he was still punished and disciplined while maintaining his innocence: "I didn't steal the keys, I *found* them."

The purloined keys were part of Alex's accelerating pattern of acting out, and the detested priest wanted to expel him from the school just before Easter. George took the train down to Ottawa, and both father and son were crying when they walked into the principal's office, at one point falling to their knees to beg the man not to kick Alex out of school.

Their tears swayed the principal, who said Alex could stay through June but that he couldn't return in the fall. That summer, Alex and his father repeated their performance, and the principal agreed to let him reenroll, but added that he'd be on probation—any more outbursts or confrontations and he'd be instantly expelled.

Alex had learned his lesson.

Even though Alex had tempered his behavior, his anger was never far from the surface. Luckily, he discovered that in addition to books and the radio, movies provided an excellent way for him to escape that feeling. And it didn't hurt that he got along with his new adviser, who, Alex recalled, "had a simple rule: you do well in class, you get privileges."

In Alex's book, that meant if he kept his grades up and no fistfights broke out between him and a priest, he could go to the movies in town as long as he had finished his homework and was back in the dorm by bedtime.

Around that time he started a journal, just jotting down his daily activities. "After three weeks, the diary consisted of nothing but the titles of movies I had seen," he said.

In addition to movies, he was also a big fan of *The Goon Show*, a British radio program from the BBC that had originally run from 1951 to 1960. The show had the air of absurdist comedy, a bit of postwar humor mixed with a pre–*Monty Python* sensibility. Comedian Spike Milligan and a young Peter Sellers starred in the show.

Alex had friends in class and at the dorms, and he liked to pal around with his buddies, going to the movies or wandering around downtown Ottawa. Because he had tamped down his wild side after his first year at the school, his classmates thought he was levelheaded and would look to him to weigh in on which side was right during a disagreement. "They thought I was the epitome of common sense," he said. But he clearly missed stirring the pot, and had to settle for standing on the sidelines, which made him feel even more alone than usual.

Besides that, his parents' separation continued to weigh heavily on him. He still saw his mother, but she seemed distracted, not fully present, which had never been an issue between them before. He sensed that something was not quite right with her, though he couldn't put his finger on it.

Alex's intuition was spot-on, because Lucille was keeping a huge secret. Shortly after she moved out, she met a man named Bill whom she quickly fell for. She was separated from George, but they were not yet divorced, so when she became pregnant with Bill's child, she panicked and did the best she could to conceal her pregnancy from Barbara and Alex, and, of course, from her soon-to-be ex-husband.

Though Bill loved her, his family was vehemently opposed to Lucille having his baby, and indeed, to any part of their relationship. So he left her and he eventually moved to Italy.

Lucille was working as a governess at the time, and when she couldn't hide her pregnancy any longer, she moved to a home for unwed mothers in Windsor, Ontario. On December 30, 1955, she gave birth to a son and named him William Vicky Trebek—using two names from Bill's family—before handing him over to a foster home.

She would keep her secret from her own family for three more decades.

As the prospect of college loomed during his senior year in prep school, Alex flailed around a bit. "I never really made plans as to what my future would be in terms of an adult," he said. He still wanted to learn about everything he possibly could, a goal that was reinforced when one day a teacher zoomed in on his best trait. "He told me never to lose my love of life," Alex recalled. Alex was thrilled that someone had noticed his deep curiosity about things, and he vowed to hold on to it at all costs.

Nevertheless, it was time to buckle down and start to

narrow the field when it came to his future. Alex had played a fair number of sports during high school, but he was never too excited about it, which ruled out athletic scholarships. Though he'd made the basketball team as a point guard, he much preferred working behind the scenes, managing the team and cheering it on.

He applied to the University of Ottawa, into which his prep school fed, and he was quickly accepted. He was still stuck when it came time to pick his major, but his precarious financial position dictated that he settle on philosophy. Philosophy classes were offered only from nine to noon each morning. (Except for Alex, all of the other philosophy majors were entering the priesthood, which meant they had to attend theology classes in the afternoon.) Alex's schedule meant he could work a full-time job in the afternoon to make enough to pay room and board and tuition, which was $500 a year, a significant amount of money at the time.

He worked at a number of odd jobs, from a sales position at a men's clothing shop to a gig at the national income tax office, handling tax returns. They were menial positions, but they paid for his education.

Despite his full workload, Alex threw himself into a wide variety of activities, just as he had done in prep school, from joining the debate team to acting in college theater productions. While acknowledging that *Othello* was a particularly difficult play for even professional stage actors to tackle, several reviewers singled him out for his performance in the role of Brabantio. Alex also produced a performance of George Bernard Shaw's play *Arms and the Man*.

Alex found that, in contrast to the priest at the boarding

school who had made his life miserable, the priests at the university and he got on quite well. One of them was Father Rene Cournoyer, who coached football. "He would hoist up his cassocks and kick the ball forty or fifty yards across the exercise yards," Alex said. Another priest—Father Jean Labbe—held out hope that Alex would decide to join the priesthood. Alex always demurred, but he recalled that "Father Labbe taught me about the finer things in life, like good cognac and a fine Cuban cigar."

In the summer of 1958, two and a half years after giving up her illegitimate son for adoption, Lucille was living in Cincinnati, working as a governess for Joseph Kanter, a local real estate developer, and his wife, Nancy Reed Kanter. Alex had just finished his freshman year of college and needed a job, and Lucille helped get him hired on the maintenance crew at one of Kanter's residential apartment buildings, mostly cleaning hallways and picking up trash. He stayed in a bare-bones apartment with only a bed and a TV, with a cardboard box serving as his dresser.

The summer was a particularly hot one, and Alex wasn't used to the extreme heat. "I'd go to my apartment for lunch and drink a gallon of lemonade because I was so thirsty," he said.

His parents' divorce became final in August 1958, and he returned to Ottawa in the fall. He plunged right back into his routine of classes and mundane jobs, but it quickly grew tedious. Alex felt that he lacked a purpose in life, and that majoring in philosophy and folding men's shirts wasn't doing anything to benefit people, or himself. He saw that the priests who were his classmates were following a higher calling, and so Alex started to entertain the idea of a life in the priesthood.

"I was going through a period where I wanted to help humanity," he said. "I wanted to be a teacher and a helper. What better way than through religion?"

He slogged through his sophomore year with one goal in mind: he'd test out his idea by spending the summer at a monastery. He later admitted it was a big mistake.

"Youngsters sometimes go to extremes," he said, firmly placing his commitment to spend three months at a Trappist monastery in that category. "I took a vow not only of poverty but of silence, but I'm not one to keep my big mouth shut, since I enjoy talking," he said. After only a month, he decided that the religious life was not for him.

He returned for his junior year no closer to figuring things out, but at least he was relieved that he knew what he *didn't* want to do. He still found college unexciting and was starting to lose interest in his studies. "It got to be boring and tiring, and I was not really into it the way I should have been," he admitted.

One day, he thought it might be a good idea to have more structure in his life, and what better institution than the military? So on a break from school, he signed up for a trial run at the Royal Military College Saint-Jean in Quebec. This time, it took only six days for him to realize that he had made a mistake.

The realization came during a routine bed-making inspection. The military requires sheets to be tucked in so tightly that a coin thrown onto them will bounce back. Alex obsessed over the task until he was sure the finished product would pass muster. When a higher-ranking cadet entered the room, he asked Alex if he had made the bed.

"I did, sir!"

"That's really good. What's your name?"

"Trebek, sir!"

"Has anybody torn up your bed yet?"

"No, sir!"

Sheets and blankets and pillows went flying as the cadet undid all of Alex's hard work. And while protocol might have dictated that recruits must be torn down before they could be built up, Alex instantly lost his passion for the military. "Don't give me that bullshit," he said about the event years later. "I can take an order without you behaving like a jerk." He packed his bags and left.

Alex's resolve to put himself to the test of military discipline might in fact have been weakened shortly before he arrived at Saint-Jean, when he had met a woman he fell hard for. "The thought of being away from her for this extended period of time [didn't help]," he admitted. But they stopped seeing each other shortly after he returned to Ottawa.

After military college, Alex was frustrated that he still hadn't found his purpose in life. Perhaps to compensate for his indecision—and to fill the gap—he signed up to play football and basketball, but admittedly he wasn't that into them. He also dabbled in hockey—practically a Canadian birthright— though he didn't get fanatical about it like his fellow students and actually took some pride in his contrarian attitude. "Canadians can do other things than play hockey," he joked. But after just a few outings on the football field, he hurt his knee during a game, which provided a handy excuse to bow out of all sports.

He still went to the movies as often as he could. He occasionally hung out with his friends, most of who preferred drinking to sitting in a dark theater. Alex would sometimes go with them to the bars, but heedful of how his father's drinking had affected his family life, he wasn't much of a drinker, though he occasionally made an exception. One day he was visited by a friend from Sudbury who liked to brag about his ability to hold his liquor. He challenged Alex to a contest. Alex wasn't terribly fond of beer, but his friend finally wore him down, and they headed out to see who could drink the most.

Back then in Canada, beer was typically served in glass bottles, either in quarts or pints. "I think I got to seven quarts and one pint while he got to eight quarts before we staggered back," Alex said. "I got hit by a car on the way home, but there was no damage to the car."

He dusted himself off and headed back to campus, chalking it up as another life experience, but still no closer to discovering his life's passion.

It was time for Alex to look for a summer job. He wanted to work days so he could keep his evenings free for a change, and he scanned the job boards at college and the want ads in the local newspaper. One day, he saw a notice for a part-time announcer at CKOY, a local radio station.

He was intrigued. He'd never before considered being on live radio, but it had to be better than getting stuck in a clothing store or a stuffy government office for the summer.

He auditioned by reading news headlines and farm reports, and thought he did a decent job; after all, he'd spent countless hours listening to radio broadcasts of all kinds.

The producer who interviewed him said that Alex had aced the audition, but there was a problem. "We feel we're one of the top stations in the country, and we wouldn't feel right hiring somebody with absolutely no experience," he told him.

Alex was disappointed, but he understood. Not long after that, he found out that the CBC—the government-run TV and radio network of Canada—was looking for a part-time announcer to fill in when on-air talent went on summer vacation. Again, he gave a great audition, and this time he was hired despite his lack of experience. He clearly had the talent, and that's all that mattered.

He continued to work part-time at the station when classes started up again in the fall, and he was flourishing at the job and proud of the work he did. He was providing news and information to people, and felt his job was important, since it affected how people went about their day. He also filled in for other announcers when they went on vacation and around the holidays. He found he had a knack for it, and he really enjoyed it.

In February of his senior year, his boss asked if he wanted to work at the station full-time as a staff announcer, which would entail a big change: in addition to working on the radio, he would also work on the TV side, which meant he had to be comfortable in front of the camera doing studio work as well as live remotes and news spots.

Alex was thrilled at the offer, and said yes, with a caveat:

first he wanted to finish out the semester and get his degree. His boss agreed, and increased his radio hours in the meantime; he would now work from 6 P.M. to midnight doing station breaks, plus reading news, weather, and sports reports.

One day, as Alex was getting ready to graduate from college—the first in his family to do so—he was digging through a box of papers and found the note he had written to himself when he was twelve, back before his family had fallen apart.

A pilot, a doctor, or prime minister of Canada.

He pulled out the piece of paper and stared at it.

Pilot. "I realized that I could be a pilot no matter what occupation I was pursuing—all I had to do was take flying lessons," he said. He crossed it off the list.

Doctor. At university, Alex had grown close to Father Lorenzo Danis, who worked with the medical school, and who thought he would make a fine physician. But Alex had no desire to spend any more time in the classroom, so he put a big X through the word.

Prime minister. He already knew he couldn't be a politician if he continued to work in broadcasting. Besides, he had interviewed enough politicians by now to know that they had to watch what they said, and he had no interest in that. He struck it from the list.

Gone were pilot, doctor, and prime minister. He was an announcer, but that felt too bland, and not ambitious enough.

So instead he wrote down *Entertainer.*

He *was* entertaining people, after all—in addition to informing them about the things that affected their world. His current job provided him with the opportunity to learn new things every day, and to help people. What more could he ask for?

And more important, who knew where it could lead?

Entertainer sounded great. He underlined the word for good measure.

He was on his way.

2

REACHING FOR THE TOP

After Alex's graduation in 1961, the producers at the CBC put him to work. He was a handsome new face, and producers thought he'd attract a younger audience to the network.

He was hired as a staff announcer at $8,855.41 a year in Canadian dollars. He pitched in wherever they needed him, which was everywhere, from sports to news and farm reports, and the occasional live remote for Red Cross blood drives, where he'd interview local radio and TV personalities to entice locals to come in and donate blood. He also reported stories that occasionally made it onto the national network.

Alex's facility in both English and French also put him in demand, since he could work for both the CBC's French and English networks; during special live events like orchestra concerts and classical ballet performances, they'd book Alex to handle the commentary in both languages rather than use two different announcers.

He loved the flexibility and the wide range of assignments. "I didn't have a chance to get bored with the regular staff announcing tasks," he said, adding that he also served as host for several dramatic performances that featured well-known directors and actors, like fellow Canadian William Shatner.

Because he was still the new kid on the block—and garnering many plum assignments that had previously gone to veteran announcers on the staff—a few coworkers didn't neglect to hide their jealousy. And they didn't hesitate to prank him, either.

Newscasters and on-air personalities from Walter Cronkite to Rachel Maddow have long subscribed to the adage "Business on Top, Party on the Bottom" when it comes to dressing for newscasts; in other words, only your top half has to look presentable, because that's the only part of the body that appears on camera. So once Alex started to do frequent newscasts, he soon followed suit, wearing a dress shirt, tie, and jacket—and shorts—when he was on the air.

During one newscast, another announcer, having just reported on several community events, introduced Alex's segment—after, unbeknownst to Alex, having secretly arranged with the cameraperson to slowly run the camera around the set to reveal Alex delivering the news while wearing shorts and flip-flops.

Alex also got the chance to entertain early on when he was selected to costar with two other staffers on *Carte Blanche*, a new variety show featuring local singers and celebrities. Alex sang "Brush Up Your Shakespeare" from the musical *Kiss Me, Kate*. The show had the odd airtime of 11:37 P.M. on Wednesdays.

But several days later, reviewer Andrew Webster struck

a sour note after watching several episodes, calling it "a tiresomely conventional patchwork of showbiz songs, self-conscious skits and dances." And he called one skit "cheese-cake satire," adding that Alex was "playing straight-man to a heavily made-up chap portraying a chunky Jane Tarzan."

Alex wasn't worried—he was too busy and in demand. When he wasn't doing remotes or reading farm reports, he was—what else?—binging on movies, both old and new. Two films in particular made a lasting impression on him.

The Razor's Edge, starring Tyrone Power, came out in 1946, and when Alex saw it years later he was struck by the story of a World War I vet and the struggles he encountered after returning home from the war. "He was searching for the truth in life, and I, too, was trying to find an answer in life for some things I had seen," he said.

The other movie was *Lonely Are the Brave*, a 1962 film starring Kirk Douglas. Alex said, "It's about an individualist who doesn't want to be fettered by modern society and gets into trouble as a result," to which he could definitely relate. Alex was twenty-two when the movie came out, and he was filled with compassion for Douglas's character.

Alex was absolutely in his element at the CBC, creating a new life of his own. He was building a name for himself—and a career—and having fun while learning the ins and outs of doing live radio and TV.

Higher-ups at the network had already noticed his talent, flair, and versatility, and just eighteen months after he'd graduated from college, network executives asked if he wanted to transfer to network headquarters in Toronto, a bigger market and a much more cosmopolitan city than Ottawa, with more visibility and opportunities.

Of course, he said yes.

Alex started his new job in a studio that he later described as "the size of an enlarged closet." But, he added, "It was paradise."

Since Alex was the youngest—and newest—on-air employee, the network put him to work on a show that nobody else wanted: it went on the air at five o'clock in the morning. His last regular stint in Ottawa had been a late-night newscast, so it made for quite an adjustment. But Alex was determined to shine, and he dutifully set his alarm clock for 4:15 every morning. (He lived just three blocks from the studio.)

His coworkers had their doubts, and they even started a betting pool to guess the first day that Alex would miss the alarm and sleep in. Though he continued to reassure the staff, he nevertheless decided to cover his bases by taping a thirty-minute "safety tape," which provided a half hour of generic programming to serve as a buffer until he could get to the station.

His first show was in September and went off without a hitch. Every morning, he would show up in plenty of time to settle into the booth. But one morning in mid-November, he woke up to see that the clock read 5:03. He leapt out of bed, threw on some clothes, and turned on the radio to hear the safety tape.

But it wasn't his own dulcet tones coming from the speaker, it was someone else's. Something was definitely wrong, and he hurried to the CBC, noticing that the streets were unusually congested for such an early hour. He dashed upstairs to the studio just as a coworker was coming downstairs. His colleague asked him if he was covering a night shift for someone.

Suddenly, it all made sense. Earlier that afternoon, Alex had lain down to take a nap, and when he woke up, his clock said 5:03 P.M., not A.M. "That's when I decided that I should start getting to bed before one o'clock in the morning," he said.

His newscasting and anchor skills aside, there was another reason why the CBC had brought Alex to Toronto. The TV show *American Bandstand* had been a hit from the time it started airing on the other side of the border in 1957, and executives at the CBC had taken notice. They thought Alex's youth would be an asset on a new music show aimed at a teen audience, a Canadian variation on *Bandstand*.

Fellow announcer Alan Hamel was four years older than Alex and had taped the pilot show for *Music Hop*. It had tested well with viewers, but Hamel was already hosting an afternoon program for kids called *Razzle Dazzle*, and since *Music Hop* would also air in the afternoon, the station needed a different young host for the show.

Music Hop went on the air in October 1963 with Alex as host. The format of the weekly show was similar to that of *Bandstand*, with a wide range of Canadian singers performing current hits. Many of the singers and musicians who appeared were unknown outside Canada at the time but would go on to bigger careers later on, singers such as Anne Murray and Gordon Lightfoot—he appeared on the show several times— and the band Creedence Clearwater Revival.

However, unlike *Bandstand*, *Music Hop* was performed live, without cue cards or a script. "If I made a mistake, there was no saving me," said Alex. "I just had to live with it."

On one occasion, he was getting ready to present that week's most popular song, and he couldn't come up with the name. "I turned to the piano player and said 'Norm!' and he gave me the title," said Alex. When it happened again not too long after that, he again asked Norm for the name of the song, but he drew a blank as well. So Alex introduced the song by saying, "Whatever it is, here's somebody to sing it."

It didn't take long for Alex to become known as the Canadian Dick Clark, though at first his hair was so thick and wavy that it presented a problem; while it might have been fine for a smaller audience back in Ottawa, he was now presenting to a nationwide audience and image was more important. Since it was the early 1960s and he was working for a network run by the Canadian government, he had to opt for a more strait-laced, slightly conservative image. So a hairdresser came to the studio every week to straighten his hair.

Reviews for *Music Hop* were generally positive. One critic wrote that Alex "keeps the show on balance. He seems able to keep things swinging, but his natural presence comes through so any parent watching could come away feeling the future of the world isn't that bleak after all."

But not every reviewer felt that way. One cranky columnist first panned a teenage girl who appeared on the show—"She went flat more often than a child trying to skate for the first time"—before she put Alex in her crosshairs.

"Alex Trebek left Ottawa to host this CBC show for the swing set, and he's trying to create the image that he's a

swinger," wrote Sandy Gardiner in *The Ottawa Journal*. "He's
not and it's obvious . . . For the first time in my life, the show
made me enjoy commercials."

Ouch. But despite the occasional negative review, the show
evolved over time and would run with Alex as host for another
four seasons.

A month after *Music Hop* premiered, on November 22, 1963,
Alex was working the afternoon shift on the radio, announcing news and sports, when a news flash came across the wire
from Dallas, Texas. President John F. Kennedy had just been
assassinated, and it was up to Alex to announce his death.
He made it through the broadcast, his voice wavering, and
recalled that standard CBC practice when a prominent world
figure died was to postpone regularly scheduled programs
and news and instead play somber classical music pieces all
day, with news updates interjected every fifteen minutes.

So Alex chose the music and checked the wire for any news
about the president, but then he reconsidered. This was a major world news story, and he believed Canadians deserved to
be kept abreast of everything, as it happened. "The tragedy
of the American president's assassination was far too important and the CBC had a responsibility to our listeners to keep
them informed," he said. So he approached his boss to plead
his case, and his boss concurred. Over the next few days, right
through the president's funeral, the CBC broadcast, around
the clock, news and analysis from the major radio and TV
networks in the United States.

Alex was saddened by the news, of course, but thrilled that his
news judgment had made an impact. He started to provide his

producers with more input and ideas, which were occasionally implemented. He spent the next couple of years honing his skills as host of *Music Hop*, anchoring the morning-drive show, and continuing to fill in wherever he was needed.

Occasionally the network would pick up a show that had successfully launched in a smaller market and rejigger it to appeal to a national audience. *Reach for the Top*, a quiz show featuring high school students as contestants, had been a hit in Vancouver since 1961, and the Toronto station started running a local edition four years later. Ratings were high, and so the network decided to relaunch it as a nationwide show in 1966. Alex was a natural choice as host for the national broadcast, since there wasn't much of an age difference between him and the contestants. He took to the show like a fish to water.

"It felt like the right fit for me," he said. While he disliked many popular TV game shows of the day, like *Supermarket Sweep* and *Let's Make a Deal*, he was partial to shows that tested the intelligence and knowledge of both contestants and viewers. "I like shows that require the contestants to be bright—they have to know something; it's not just a question of luck."

Plus, he said, *Reach for the Top* "was great training for what I would wind up doing many, many years later," though the competition could be more cutthroat than anything Alex would ever confront on *Jeopardy!* After one show had ended, the losing team thought that Alex had thrown the game to the other side, and they surrounded him and started yelling. "They were [acting] like a lynch mob," he said. Fortunately, a teacher intervened and broke up the fight. "I was genuinely frightened."

On the flip side, at the same time he was hosting *Reach*, Alex started to preside over shows that featured the sport of curling. In addition to providing play-by-play for events in Canada, he went overseas to cover international competitions. One year he traveled to Scotland for the annual World Curling Championships, and attended several banquets, where he noticed that there was a bottle of Scotch at each table. "I soon realized it was there because you needed it to eat the haggis," he said.

He also hosted an afternoon variety show called *Afternoon*, which aired in front of an audience from the Colonnade Theatre in Toronto between 1 and 2 P.M. The show was patterned along the lines of a late-night talk show, complete with a short opening monologue, live band, and interviews with celebrities who had a movie or book to promote. One of the regulars on the show was a writer and producer named Alan Thicke.

Afternoon didn't last long, but a friendship developed between Alan and Alex. They started to hang together outside of the show until 1970, when Thicke moved to California because he felt his opportunities in Canada were; afterwards, he'd occasionally returned to his home country for different projects.

Alex wasn't happy his friend was leaving, but he kept tabs on Thicke's career.

Alex continued to appear everywhere. "I did everything, at one time replacing every announcer in every possible job," he said.

In the spring of 1969, he agreed to host a new half-hour

game show called *Strategy*, though he had his doubts, because it was a show where winning didn't rely on raw brainpower as it did on *Reach for the Top*. But just as was the case with *Music Hop*, the show's producers thought his age would help attract a younger audience to the show.

In the game, two couples stood on the outside of a large circle that looked like a dartboard, with Alex at the center. He'd read out questions and the couple who gave the right answer would move one space closer to Alex, though they could also use their win to move to a space that would block their opponents from reaching the center first. A ticking clock ratcheted up the tension, and if no team reached Alex first, the one nearest him won first prize, usually a washer and dryer or a freezer. There were no returning champions, so each game started with a new set of contestants.

The show lasted only six months, but Alex didn't mind, since there was always another new show or program for him to do.

Besides, he had a full life outside the studio as well. Many of his coworkers who had been at the CBC for decades, not to mention the television stars and celebrities he regularly interviewed, lived in large elegant homes and drove expensive cars. While he appreciated their lifestyle, he knew they were way out of his league, money-wise. But he could afford a house that needed work, and since his uncles had taught him the ins and outs of home repair, he felt confident that he could handle anything the house threw at him. Besides, he had learned in childhood that it was far better to buy a house than to rent; it was like having money in the bank, and you couldn't get evicted.

So instead of renting a modern apartment as most eligible bachelors in town would have done, Alex bought a three-story fixer-upper on George Street, a few minutes from the CBC studios. The house was in such bad shape that he could have easily worked full-time on it. But since he already had a time-consuming job, he convinced his uncle Arnold from up in Sudbury to come to Toronto and paint the house. Even though Arnold was in his fifties and had slowed down somewhat, Alex knew he would finish the job in half the time it would take anyone else. "The great thing about Uncle Arnold is that he was ambidextrous," said Alex. "He'd sit on a stool or on the windowsill, cigarette in one hand and paintbrush in the other, and paint the house." He'd then switch hands before moving on to the next section without having to adjust the ladder.

After work on the George Street house was finished, Alex decided to build a ski chalet in Collingwood on Georgian Bay, a section of Lake Huron that is sometimes called the sixth Great Lake. The region, located just about a hundred miles northwest of Toronto, is popular as a vacation destination for people in the city.

He frequently needed to haul building supplies from the city, but he opted against buying a pickup truck in favor of a 1965 Cadillac convertible, which could easily carry pieces of lumber up to twelve feet in length because the car was almost nineteen feet long. "I'd unzip the rear window and set one end on the dashboard, and the other end never stuck out beyond the rear bumper," he said.

Back in Toronto, Alex started to entertain regularly. He liked to cook—taking after his father—and give dinner parties. "Entertaining is a very simple thing," he said. "You pick the right people, get them talking, and give them some good booze."

As his visibility grew—as well as his reputation as Toronto's most eligible bachelor—reporters frequently asked about his romantic life, but Alex usually said it was a nonissue.

"I haven't met the right woman yet because I've been too busy pursuing my career to have a stable, emotional relationship with anyone," he said. But in truth, he was finding dating to be more of a hassle than anything else. Whenever he'd mention on his show where he'd gone the previous night, any woman he was dating would call him up and demand to know who else he was seeing. "That's why I end up going lots of places alone," he told reporters. In addition, when he did go out, the date had to be over by 10 P.M., given his early-morning rising time. "Any girl who dates me has time for two dates on the same night."

However, he was briefly engaged to Vanda King, a singer and pianist who appeared on *Nightcap*, a CBC variety show that aired in the mid-1960s.

"I got lucky and we didn't get married," he said. "It wouldn't have worked out. It was an infatuation for each of us, but not destined to survive."

Still, he didn't rule out marriage in the future, though he did have a few must-haves. "If and when I do tie the knot, the girl will have to be intelligent, sophisticated, and probably good-looking," he said.

Alex considered a woman's eyes to be the first point of attraction. "I was into faces more than bodies," he explained. "I was never one of those guys who said, 'Boy, look at the knockers on that girl.'" Being able to laugh at life—and themselves—as well as having the ability to cook a decent meal added bonus points.

He would be accused of coming across as a bit detached in later years, and the women he worked with—and those he dated—often said the same thing. It could have been a reaction against the onslaught of female attention he was receiving on a daily basis, or it could have been a childhood trait, a residual self-defense against being hurt by divorced parents who he felt dumped him at a boarding school. Or it could have been a little of both.

"You never really got to know Alex," said Juliette, a singer and TV host who cohosted several CBC shows with Alex. "He never gave you the feeling that he wanted you to come up and talk to him."

He could also be a bit tightfisted when it came to money, some said. "Whenever we went out to lunch, Alex would say he wasn't hungry, but he always enjoyed a little bit of everybody else's lunch," said Juliette. "We'd end up paying the bill, but Alex didn't have to because he never ordered anything."

"He's a typical Jesuit boy—he should have been a priest," said Elaine Saunders, an in-house CBC makeup artist. "He has all those Jesuitical rigidities and can be very moody. But he's extremely intelligent and was destined for success."

His coworkers often attended the dinner parties he threw at his George Street home, and Juliette was a frequent guest. On one occasion, she excused herself to go to the bathroom, where she noticed a picture of what looked like dancing couples hanging on the wall. Then she took a closer look. "They were actually all in different sexual positions," she said. "I thought, 'Oh my God, isn't this awful? Why would Alex have anything like this on the wall?' So I stole it."

No word on whether Alex noticed, or if he ever figured out who'd taken it.

After more than a decade at the CBC, Alex was a well-seasoned professional, and still jumping whenever a producer told him to jump. He still enjoyed the sheer variety of topics he covered in the course of his job, but he was starting to tire of being a kind of network lapdog, and he wanted to expand his skill set by starring in his own TV show. In his mind, this would accomplish two things: he'd be able to do more behind-the-scenes work, which would enable him to have more influence and control over the end result; and the CBC would hold him in higher regard than it currently did.

When he presented higher-ups with his ideas, they usually resisted, believing that when it came to the TV side, if it ain't broke why fix it? Besides, the CBC had always been reluctant to boost one personality over another. "The CBC believed that no performer is big or important enough to be in command of his show," said Alex Barris, a longtime fixture on CBC television through the 1950s and 1960s.

However, the network was starting to feel the pressure from smaller private TV networks that were keeping up with the times by launching more modern shows and letting their personalities take more of a starring role. CTV launched in 1961, and though its influence was small at first, CBC executives kept an eye on it. So did Alex.

In the meantime, he had to be content with serving as game-show host to couples battling ferociously over a chest freezer—his gig on *Reach for the Top* had ended—or as a side-kick to CBC veterans who had spent several decades paying their dues. In 1968 he was booked as Alex Barris's partner on *Barris & Company*, a live variety show that aired on Saturday nights at 10:30, or whenever the hockey game that preceded it had wrapped up. But Alex's restlessness was starting to show. "None of us liked the results," said Barris. "Alex seemed too snarky, too determined to assert himself, and somewhat negative about the whole show."

Barris & Company lasted only four months before it was canceled.

In the early 1970s, the stranglehold that the CBC had on national broadcasting was starting to loosen. The network was losing market share not only to CTV but to other commercial stations as well, since younger audiences viewed the government-run network as stuffy and stodgy.

CBC executives and producers finally began to shake up the schedule, but not by giving Alex his own show; instead, they insisted that he'd best serve their purposes by acting as the congenial host and presiding over softer programs like *Pick and Choose*, another game show. Probably because he was so versatile, the CBC didn't want him to stay put on any one show. For an old show that needed a boost in the ratings, they'd bring him on for a while. But then, if the ratings continued to sag, they'd pull him off and install him on another show.

While Alex enjoyed the variety, he didn't like the fact that his career was at the mercy of some stuffed shirts in the executive suite who viewed him merely as a someone who could haul in a younger audience. He wanted more control over his life and his career.

Despite his good looks and relative ease in front of the camera, in October 1971 Alex was unceremoniously yanked off the TV side and installed on a drive-time morning show on CBL-AM called *I'm Here Till 9* . . . because the show ran from 5 to 9 A.M. Station executives hoped he would pull in a hip morning crowd who'd stay tuned for the rest of the day.

With his face splashed in ads in local newspapers to promote the show, more people started to recognize him. *The Globe and Mail* described the new host as "a dashing bilingual bachelor, who can be expected to show more bounce, and thus be more like his competitors on commercial stations."

But the reality is that the show was rather bland. Despite its desire to update the format and content of its programming, the network was also aiming to homogenize all broadcasts, to make them more alike from coast to coast despite the unique identities of each province. Quoted anonymously, one CBC executive confided that they were "going back into the eighteenth century in search of an audience that isn't there anymore."

Shortly after the show debuted, the critics weighed in. "The most important part of the show has consisted almost entirely of alternating records and commercials, with a few pleasant words from Trebek to separate them," wrote *Globe and Mail* critic Blaik Kirby, and not in a flattering way.

Though the morning radio show took up a good chunk of his day, Alex still managed to host other special events and one-offs, which included horse racing events like the Queen's Plate and the Breeders' Stakes, and national beauty pageants

like the Miss Teenage Canada pageant and the Miss Central
Canada pageant.

In 1972, he served as the master of ceremonies for a television presentation of *The Sleeping Beauty* in Toronto, with
Rudolf Nureyev directing the dancers' performances. Unfortunately, there was no live orchestra; instead, conductor
George Crum had to make do by flailing his arms along to
prerecorded music.

When Alex asked members of the audience to stand and
applaud the conductor before the ballet started, there were
more than a few snickers. He frowned, folded his arms, and
in the same way he would chastise numerous *Jeopardy!* contestants in the future for muffing an easy answer, he proceeded to chide the audience of ballet aficionados. Suitably
embarrassed, they then offered up boisterous applause for
Crum's skill at leading an imaginary orchestra.

Though Alex was feeling a bit restless, his tenure at the CBC
did have one big side benefit: thanks to the big ad push to
promote his morning drive time show, it wasn't unusual for
people to stop him on the streets of Toronto and ask for an
autograph, though the most surprising place he was recognized was halfway around the world, and not for the radio
show, or for his *Reach for the Top* days, either.

He was exploring the Himalaya mountains in Nepal in
the late 1960s, and very early one morning, he had traveled
up a mountain to catch the sunrise. As he witnessed the grand
event, he saw a man tentatively approach him. He asked Alex
if he was the same guy who hosted curling shows on the CBC.

Alex was surprised to be recognized so far from home,

and for curling of all things. He nodded and said he was indeed who the man thought he was, and the man went on his way, leaving Alex to continue relishing the sunrise . . . as well as finding a fan in such a remote location.

"It's enjoyable being recognized," he said. "It's good for your ego."

A year after Alex started his radio show, the network dropped a bomb. In October 1972, the CBC announced it would convert all of its local early-morning shows to an all-news format, and it canceled his light-music-and-talk show.

Though he'd definitely had his issues with the show, Alex wasn't happy at being dumped after all his years of loyalty. "They came up with a new format last year and now they've decided that's not what they should be doing," he complained. "They don't really know what they're doing."

It was finally time to look elsewhere. He decided to head to Los Angeles, where his friends Alan Thicke and Alan Hamel kept telling him how busy they were and how many opportunities there'd be for him if he followed. Every so often, both Alans suggested to Alex that he should head south as well, and that his opportunities for success would be limitless, but he had always shrugged off the idea, as he wasn't yet ready to leave Canada and the CBC behind.

Going to America was far from an unusual endeavor for Canadians who were itching for new challenges. "The measure of Canadian merit seems always to be checked on an American yardstick of success," said Alex Barris. "And the public attitude suggests that you don't arrive until you've left." Add to that the fascination that the entertainment industry had toward those from north of the border, which Barris referred to as an "almost mystical faith in Canadians, where they find a more receptive atmosphere than if they're from, say, Australia or Chicago."

The CBC had been his life for more than thirteen years, but he had reached his limit. His last day of work there was December 29, 1972.

3

CALIFORNIA, HERE I COME

With the help of the two Alans, Alex put out some feelers in Los Angeles, and he was thrilled to receive some requests to audition for several programs and networks. He scheduled an interview with Roone Arledge, the president of ABC Sports who had made a name for himself by launching *Wide World of Sports* and *Monday Night Football*. He wanted to talk with Alex about coming on board to host a variety of sports shows.

Though a position didn't pan out at ABC, doors were opening for Alex more quickly than he had expected. "When I first came to the United States, I was well received," he said. "Everywhere I went people said, 'Oh, you're Canadian, you're automatically a nice person.'"

As it turned out, Alan Thicke came to the rescue. After moving to California in 1970, he had quickly secured work as a writer and producer on several sitcoms and variety shows, as well as writing theme music. In 1972, he was working on the launch of a new game show called *The Wizard of Odds*, and he and the other producers had already considered and auditioned more than sixty candidates for the show, from to-tal unknowns to big stars of the time like Ed McMahon and Dick Clark. They were specifically looking for a fresh face with game-show experience who could also work without cue cards, since the show was set on a stage in the round, with numerous cameras placed at all angles. So far, it was proving to be a tall order to fill.

"Most of [the candidates] had difficulty memorizing all the details necessary to keep the show moving," explained Lin Bolen, vice president for daytime TV at NBC, who had a take-no-prisoners reputation and was generally considered to be the inspiration for Faye Dunaway's character in the movie *Network*.

Thicke remembered that Alex hadn't used cue cards on the CBC show *Strategy*, so he called him to see if he'd be interested in the job. At the time, the average game-show viewer in the United States skewed female and older, and Thicke thought that a younger host who wasn't overexposed to the American market would help the show build a follow-ing among younger viewers.

So did Lin Bolen. "Our hosts are young. We think that's what women want to see," she said.

When Thicke called about the opportunity, Alex was in-trigued but a bit hesitant. Despite his desire for a new start, he hadn't moved to the States yet since he knew there were no guarantees. But Alan was so convinced that Alex was the right fit that the very next day he flew to Toronto, where he gave Alex a crash course on the rules of the game. They performed some mock run-throughs on a cobbled-together stage set so Alex could get comfortable with the rules and the timing, and the next day they headed to New York for another dry run—but this time they dragged people in from the street and into a meeting room at the New York Hilton to play a few rounds so they could test how the show played in the real world.

When the mock game was over, Alex flew back to Toronto, landing just in time to catch the last half of a hockey game. When he unlocked the door to his apartment, the phone was ringing. He picked it up, exhausted from the nonstop pace of the last few days. It was Alan on the other end, asking him to come to California to tape a pilot.

Alex flew to Los Angeles a few days later.

As the plane touched down at the airport in Los Angeles, Alex couldn't stop grinning. He was ready for a fresh start and determined to do whatever it took to win the job. Plus, he loved Southern California.

"I felt at home in Los Angeles," he said. "In fact, I felt this way the first time I visited."

But at the audition, Alex's nerves almost got the better of him. "I was so nervous I nearly threw up," he admitted years later.

Despite his nerves, he got the job. He was excited, ecstatic, and, yes, still a bundle of nerves about what lay ahead. Not long after Bolen made the formal offer, she pulled him aside. "How do you feel about your mustache?" she asked.

Though he'd started his broadcast career at the CBC with a more clean-cut look, as the 1960s progressed and politics—and fashion—became more radical, Trebek's sense of personal style had followed along with the changing times. Canadian viewers had long been accustomed to seeing him flit from show to show with a bushy mustache and a full head of hair that some referred to as an Afro. In other words, he more resembled a star in a grainy 1970s porn movie than a trustworthy broadcaster and game-show host.

He was a bit taken aback at Bolen's question, but decided to stand his ground. "Very strongly," he replied.

She nodded, and they left it at that. He would become the first game-show host in twelve years—since Groucho Marx's reign on *You Bet Your Life*, which aired on television from 1950 to 1961—to wear a mustache.

Alex signed a thirteen-week contract, which was a typical trial run for a new game show at the time. But when he accepted the job, he had a secret. Despite his frustration with the powers that be at the CBC, Alex had gotten used to the emotional security of having a regular job for the last twelve years. It had provided him with a good degree of financial security as well: he owned a house in downtown Toronto, he had built himself a ski chalet, and he entertained regularly.

Plus, as an admitted workaholic, he rarely took a real vacation when he was at the CBC. So when he started at *Wizard*, he had built up four months of leave time. He didn't quit his CBC job, just in case the NBC show didn't make it past the first thirteen weeks. "I wasn't taking a chance; I wasn't burning all my bridges," he said. That way he could also tell himself that he gave it a good chance and if it didn't work out, he could hightail it back to Toronto and pick up where he left off.

So he headed south to begin taping the show. He moved in with Alan Thicke, who later compared their living situation to the one in *The Odd Couple*, a hit TV sitcom at the time starring Jack Klugman as slob Oscar Madison and Tony Randall as neat freak Felix Unger. "[Alex] was the tidy one," said Thicke.

Thicke actually wrote and sang the theme song for *Wizard:*

> *Who's the fellow every day*
> *Gives a bundle away?*

The Wizard of Odds debuted on July 17, 1973, and was essentially a show for fans of math and statistics. An NBC press release described it this way: "The game takes place primarily in the audience, with Trebek choosing contestants at random and asking them questions which test their judgment of national odds, averages, and possibilities, like 'How many times a day does the average American husband kiss his wife?'"

Alex—aka "The Wizard"—also asked contestants to pick the word in a series that didn't belong, in what was essentially a version of "One of these things is not like the others." At the end of each round, the winner would select a prize from behind a window that was either unlocked or locked. If it was unlocked, winners would receive the prize featured in the window. But if it was locked, they'd lose everything they had won so far in the game. They also had the option to stop and keep whatever prizes they had accumulated and walk away.

During the bonus round, Alex gave clues containing a number, like "The Three Stooges" or "The number of weeks in a year." After all of the clues were read, the contestant had to choose the four of them that when added up would be less than, say, a random figure like 262.

The show was fast-paced and kept viewers glued to the

TV, but with thousands of different mathematical possibilities, glitches were common. On one episode, the contestant missed the correct number by one point. But Alex thought something didn't sound right, so he recalculated the numbers and announced that the contestant was correct after all. "The math doesn't work," he told the contestant. "We made a mistake, and I don't think you ought to be punished for our mistake. So I'm going to give you the car anyway." The audience whooped and cheered along with the contestant.

But as Alex headed backstage, the show's producer, Burt Sugarman, stopped him to fill him in on a bit of game-show policy. When someone—host *or* contestant—makes a mistake, said Sugarman, it's customary to pause taping and rerecord the show. "Next time you notice that we've screwed up, we'll just stop tape and rectify it," he warned. "Don't give the car away."

Unfortunately, it's impossible to find clips of the show online or off; throughout the 1960s and '70s, it was common policy at television networks to erase, or "wipe," videotapes of old shows, since tape was expensive and required a lot of storage space. New shows were recorded over the erased shows ad infinitum until the tape began to disintegrate. This was particularly true for game shows and other daytime programs, since they weren't considered to be as valuable as nighttime shows, which had higher viewership and advertising dollars, bigger budgets, and funds available to purchase new videotape for each episode.

After a few weeks, *Wizard* had done so well in the ratings that the network picked it up for six more months. That's when Alex officially quit his job at the CBC, sold his house in Canada, and hired a moving van to move all of his stuff to California.

The Canadian TV critics who had mostly cheered Alex on over the last decade, viewing him as a homegrown hero, didn't take it well. They were understandably miffed when he rewarded their loyalty by skipping out to the States. And since *The Wizard of Odds* was also shown in Canada, these jilted reviewers didn't hold back. Blaik Kirby, who had long been a fan of Alex's multifaceted talents at the CBC, called the show "as bad as any of the game shows and perhaps worse than most. Trebek has the right handsome good looks and does his job passably though unimpressively. Surely before long his embarrassment will show through."

But Alex was unperturbed. He was on his way.

Alex was thrilled with his new life. He was making more money than he had at the CBC, he had his own game show, and he was ecstatic to be living in Los Angeles, surrounded by lush greenery and great weather.

But there was a fly in the ointment: once the show was given the go-ahead, United States immigration officials told Alex that he had to get a work permit in order to keep hosting it. At the time, it wasn't easy for Canadian citizens to receive one: the U.S. economy was in a severe recession, partly caused by rising oil prices and the government's financial burden as the Vietnam War dragged on. The unemployment rate had ballooned as a result, which meant that many Americans were finding it hard to get a job, and that non–U.S. citizens faced a big obstacle, since they had to prove they had unique skills that were hard to find among American workers.

The unique skill that Alex was able to tout was his memory. Plus, *Wizard* required a host to work without cue cards, which he had honed back at the CBC. The producers lobbied hard for hiring him, stressing that he had a photographic memory—which Alex would admit years later was not true. "It was the hook they used to get me a work permit, but actually I was just able to memorize a lot of stuff," he said.

Immigration authorities granted him permission to work in the United States, and he breathed a sigh of relief.

While Alex was clearly enjoying being the host of a successful American game show, he had always viewed it as a springboard to other gigs where he could use his other talents, like producing or maybe even acting. But for the time being, he was happy he was able to help shape the show.

"We're trying to make it more challenging [by] getting away from questions like 'What percentage of men in the country wear undershirts?'" he said.

In addition, while he loved the land and the weather, he was still uncertain about the people, and he began to despair of ever fitting in with Hollywood society. "I was not a player," he admitted, and despite appearances to the contrary, he admitted that he actually didn't date that often back in Toronto. "I was a shy, small-town Canadian kid."

The smooth transition to Hollywood made by Alan Hamel—who would marry actress Suzanne Somers a few years later—only underscored Trebek's feeling of being on the outside looking in. "I always thought he fit right in to this society," Alex said of Hamel. "I never felt like I belonged."

Despite his awkwardness, Alex gamely started to make an effort to socialize. But he didn't have to make the rounds of high-wattage Hollywood cocktail parties and red-carpet events; instead he appeared as an up-and-comer on daytime talk shows like *The Dinah Shore Show*, and started to play in a variety of celebrity golf and tennis tournaments to help raise money for charity. He had always looked for ways to give back to the less fortunate, and he was thrilled when he could do so.

A number of members of the old-time Hollywood establishment took notice of the new arrival, including publicist Richard Gully, who had worked for legendary movie producer Jack Warner. Gully liked to host regular get-togethers for clients—of course, he'd alert the local media and gossip columnists—by booking a table at a hot Beverly Hills restaurant called The Bistro. "He often needed single guys to fill out the table," said Alex. In addition, *Wizard* producer Burt Sugarman was an avid backgammon player and welcomed Alex to his frequent games. These invitations suited Alex well, since they didn't require him to make the first move.

But mingling with Hollywood's movers and shakers in the 1970s meant drugs of all kinds were often a part of the scene. Though Alex had mostly limited himself just to drinking wine back in Canada, one day he tried cocaine at a party. Someone gestured at a line of white powder on a mirror with a couple of straws, and urged him to give it a try. "I inhaled, and it burned my nose," he said, and he never tried it again.

Upon the advice of a friend, he also tried smoking marijuana for an arthritic shoulder, but it didn't have any effect.

However, a Malibu party one Friday night led to a totally different outcome. "I love chocolate," said Alex, so he ate four or five brownies without knowing they were laced with ample amounts of hash. "They put me to bed Friday night because I was almost comatose." He stayed in bed all day Saturday and became somewhat conscious on Sunday, but he wasn't able to finally head home until Monday morning.

With a new job in a new country, Alex was beginning to think that perhaps the tide had turned, that he could finally relax. As if to make up for a childhood filled with instability and marked by poverty, Alex thrust himself headlong into buying things that he could never have afforded back in Canada. He had left his Cadillac in Toronto, and bought his first California car, a Volkswagen Thing, a convertible dune buggy that was popular among surfers. Before long, he traded the Thing for an Italia Spyder sports car.

It needed some work, so just as he had done with his house back in Toronto, he rolled up his sleeves and got busy refreshing the interior and laying down new carpet.

Since Alex realized that part of California culture involved seeing and being seen, the next car he sprung for was a 1956 Bentley Mulliner Park Ward convertible. It cost him $34,000—the equivalent of $177,000 in 2020. Even in a land of stunning cars, the Bentley clearly stood out. One day Alex was at a stoplight when basketball great Wilt Chamberlain stopped next to him in a new white Cadillac convertible. "Wilt looked over at me and at my car and said, 'Fine-looking car.' And I looked at the blonde lady sitting next to him and said, 'Good-looking companion.'" Then the light changed and they parted ways.

However, in time Alex found the Bentley to be a bit impractical, so he sold it for a 1956 Jaguar XK140 MC, a more understated British roadster.

Back in Canada, Alex had started to date Elaine Callei, a former Playboy Bunny who went by the name Teddy Howard for a couple of years. She was born in Columbus, Ohio, and had moved to Toronto in the late 1960s. She was hosting a daily TV talk show when she and Alex met in the early 1970s, and she had the distinction of being censured by the Canadian Radio-television and Telecommunications Commission when she invited Xaviera Hollander—the author of *The Happy Hooker*, a memoir about her life as a madam and call girl—onto her talk show.

When Alex moved to California, Elaine followed him. Soon after, they decided to get married. At the very least, since Elaine was an American citizen, Alex thought that the marriage might prevent any future employment issues for him. He also adopted Elaine's six-year-old daughter, Nicky, from her previous marriage.

They scheduled their wedding for September 25, 1974, and he, Elaine, and Nicky moved into a house next door to where the late comedian Ernie Kovacs had lived. Kovacs's widow, Edie Adams, still lived there, and befriended them. She wanted to sell her husband's wine collection, so she asked

Alex if he would take a look. He had mostly limited himself to basic wines like Mateus and Cabernet back in Toronto, but when he researched the contents of Kovacs's cellar, he was impressed by the breadth and value of the collection, and came up with some numbers for Adams.

Unbeknownst to Alex, Elaine had already approached Edie and offered to buy the entire collection for Alex for Christmas, which launched his interest in wine, including a sideline in buying and trading wines with other collectors and wine shop owners.

Unfortunately, all was not well. Despite its early promising start, the audience for *Wizard* started to drop after a few months, and the last show aired on June 28, 1974. Alex perhaps started to wonder if he should have acted so hastily in quitting the CBC.

But Alan Thicke wasn't going to let his good friend move back to Canada so quickly, and put him in touch with a producer who was looking for a host for a new game show called *High Rollers*. Alex didn't even have time to take a brief vacation—not that he would have, given his workaholic tendencies—because he started his new job three days after his last day of taping *Wizard*.

In *High Rollers*, which debuted on July 1, 1974, the numbers 1 to 9 were displayed on an electronic board; the goal was for all of the numbers to be eliminated by the roll of a pair of dice. Cohost Ruta Lee—best known for her role in the 1954 movie *Seven Brides for Seven Brothers*—rolled the dice, and the outcome would determine which numbers were removed; for instance, if a player rolled a 1 and a 4, she could choose to remove the 5, or a 2 and a 3, or a 4 and a 1, depending upon which numbers remained on the board. In one round, Alex would ask a question and the contestant who answered correctly would win control of the dice and decide which numbers to delete; a prize was under each number. In the other, a player would roll the dice and if the entire board was cleared, she'd win a prize.

High Rollers was years ahead of its peers. It relied heavily on lights and electronics going off, predating the use of computers on game shows. But malfunctions abounded, and taping had to stop whenever the wrong light flashed, or when no light flashed at all.

High Rollers was produced by Heatter-Quigley, the company that also produced *Hollywood Squares*. Each Christmas, the company flew everyone from their various game shows— hosts and celebrities and their spouses, along with production staff—to some tropical paradise for a week. One year, the trip was to Montego Bay, Jamaica, and Alex and Elaine made the jaunt.

The group contained a who's who of TV talent of the time: Marcia Wallace from *The Bob Newhart Show*, Karen Valentine from *Room 222*, and Rue McClanahan, who'd later star on *The Golden Girls*. Of course, all the regular luminaries from *Hollywood Squares* were also there: Paul Lynde, Rose Marie, Vincent Price, and Jonathan Winters. Host Peter Marshall would later say of the trip, "Maybe the moon was in the wrong place, but almost every couple on that trip barely made it through still speaking to each other."

Alex and Elaine were clearly included in that category. *Hollywood Squares* was on NBC, and as head of daytime programming at the network, Lin Bolen—who had hired Alex for *Wizard*—had come along on the trip. "Her concept of a good show was a great set with an emcee in an open shirt," Marshall would later quip.

At one point, Bolen cornered Alex and stressed that he should hide his marital status in order to build up his fan base. Needless to say, Elaine wasn't crazy about the idea, and they flew back to Los Angeles with the rest of the crowd on New Year's Day with a cloud between them.

Clearly, Lin Bolen had gotten the upper hand, because in one interview from 1975—the year after his wedding—Alex told an interviewer that he almost got married to move to the United States. "But I didn't have to do anything quite that drastic," he fibbed.

Putting on a false public face was only one of the issues in his marriage. "I didn't know what was expected of me as a husband," he admitted years later. "Elaine and I were both too reluctant to give up our respective points of view, nor were we willing to compromise."

Despite its effect on his marriage, Alex was happy he'd gone on the trip: he was still uncomfortable with the Hollywood social circuit, but he felt like he'd made great strides in Jamaica, becoming friends with stars he'd watched and admired for years. "I've never felt very much like a celebrity. I'm an ordinary Joe, and *Hollywood Squares* was the highlight of daytime television for me. And now I'm one of them," he marveled.

4

A VERY DEPRESSED MONK

High Rollers lasted almost two full years before it was canceled in June 1976. But just as before, another game show materialized right away.

Alex was hired by Goodson-Todman, a rival game-show production company. Producer Mark Goodson was highly respected in the business, and known for some of the most well-loved game shows, bringing them first to radio and then TV, including *What's My Line?*, *Beat the Clock*, *The Price Is Right*, and *To Tell the Truth*. He was looking for a host for a new show called *Double Dare* who could do more than just congratulate winners and console losers; he wanted a host who was both personable *and* cerebral, which was apparently hard to come by in Hollywood. The powerhouse producer quickly recognized that Trebek would excel on the show.

Double Dare launched in late 1976. The format featured three players in isolation booths who answered a variety of questions of increasing difficulty based on short clues. The winner proceeded to a bonus round where she was pitted against three Ph.D.s in their own isolation booths. The producers thought it best to offset the show's focus on brainpower with some glamour, but Alex later confided that he thought the tuxedos he had to wear on the show were pretty hideous.

Though he had always relished an intellectual challenge, on camera or off, even Alex admitted that he thought *Double Dare* was too challenging, and therefore not a good fit for daytime TV. "It was too tough for the room," he said.

The show lasted only four months, but Alex's next job was already waiting in the wings. The only thing was, it was waiting in the country he had left a few short years earlier.

He returned to Canada to host *Stars on Ice*, a new weekly variety show on the commercial network CTV. The show featured a cast of professional skaters performing dance routines, as well as the occasional guest star with a movie or TV show to promote.

Alex was excited about the show and about returning to his home turf, even though he had to commute each week from Los Angeles. He had grown up skating, as most Canadian children do, but he considered himself to be more utilitarian at the sport than elegant.

The gig removed him from a stagnating job market as well as a stagnant marriage, if only temporarily, and he had a blast. "I go back home and schmooze with my friends and have a real good time and get paid for it," he marveled.

In the middle of the *Stars on Ice* run, Alex was hired as host of *The $128,000 Question*, a reboot of *The $64,000 Question*, a show that had run from 1955 to 1958 before getting caught up in the quiz-show scandals of the time, which involved certain players being provided with answers in advance. The show had been pulled off the air and hadn't appeared in a revamped version until 1976, when it relaunched with Alex's fellow Canadian Mike Darow.

The first season was shot in New York, but producers decided to air the second season from Toronto. Since Alex was already hosting *Stars on Ice*, he ended up spending more time in Canada, but as was the case with his previous shows, *Question* lacked legs; it was canceled after less than a year.

If he was entertaining any notions of returning to Canada permanently, Alex kept them to himself—after all, Elaine didn't accompany him on most of his trips north. But his marriage was clearly showing the strain of his absences, as well as the financial strain.

Of course, basic incompatibility could have also played a role. But he had long ago accepted that he had committed to a highly volatile career path where there were never any guarantees, believing that despite the odds one day all of his hard work and commitment to the business would eventually pay off. "You have to pay your dues," he told a newspaper reporter in 1979. "Otherwise you'll have difficulty keeping things in proper perspective."

Whenever he was tempted to give in to the depression that occasionally swirled around him, he recalled a chat he had one day with producer Bob Noah on the set of *High Rollers*. "Never turn down a job," Noah had told him. "We're on thirteen-week renewals, and you never know when the next job is going to come up."

Alex filed that away. "Whenever somebody offers me a job, if I like the work, I accept it," he said.

This was the pattern for many game-show hosts, since most shows followed the same schedule of taping a full week's worth of five episodes in one day, which left a lot of time to accept gigs on the side, like hosting a sports event or awards show or even a Junior League banquet for some extra money and visibility.

Adding more plates to spin had been in Alex's blood from the beginning; after all, he'd started off doing it at the CBC, hosting everything from rip-and-read newscasts to quiz and music shows, and filling in on unfamiliar beats, like opera or travel shows, when someone went on vacation.

His sense of career whiplash continued when Hollywood called again, this time with plans to relaunch *High Rollers* in the spring of 1978, but this time without Ruta Lee as cohost, since the producers thought that having the contestants roll their own dice would inject the show with more energy.

He signed on for the job, but the reboot lasted less than two years, and soon Alex was out of work again. And this time around, no game-show producer offered him another job for over a year.

This time his extended unemployment was a definite strain on his marriage. "Even though I tried to stay busy, even emceeing supermarket openings to make a buck, there were weeks and months when I didn't have a dime," he admitted.

For Elaine, it was the last straw. Through the years, she had patiently stood by Alex during his various ups and downs, both career- and money-wise, but by 1980 she'd had enough and wanted a divorce. Alex struggled mightily with the fallout. "I don't like to fail at things, and to me, marriage is the biggest and most important thing a man can fail at, except for fatherhood," he said. The divorce was finalized in 1981.

He received yet another blow when his father died of cancer in January 1982. Essentially, the three biggest parts of his life had died around the same time—his father, his marriage, and his career—and he couldn't keep from sinking into a serious depression. "It was the worst time of my life," he said.

Somehow he pulled himself together enough to make a couple of appearances as a guest on several game shows, and despite his own personal and financial struggles, he still thought of ways to help people who had less than he did. When he won $50,000 on *Card Sharks*, he caught up on a few bills before heading to a local appliance store to buy a load of washers and dryers to donate to several nonprofits in Los Angeles.

As part of the terms of the divorce, the house that Alex and Elaine had shared was sold, and he moved, along with just a few pieces of furniture, into a spare studio apartment, where he lived "like a very depressed monk."

Only then did he allow himself to fully succumb to his despair. "I recall resting in bed with some Colonel Sanders chicken sitting on a plate on my chest and a bottle of white wine in my hand and the television set over there," he said. "I spent a lot of evenings that way."

Eventually, a Canadian producer named Bill Armstrong approached him about hosting a new game show that was produced and taped in Vancouver, Canada, called *Pitfall*. Of course, Alex jumped at the chance, not just for the money but for the change of venue; maybe it would lift his spirits.

But just as he'd run into trouble for being a Canadian citizen when he took the hosting job at *Wizard of Odds* back in

1973, Alex soon ran into the same trouble with *Pitfall*, which required all employees to be members of ACTRA, the Alliance of Canadian Cinema, Television and Radio Artists.

He had worked on other Canadian shows since moving to the United States, and was already a member of a different organization known as the Canadian Performers Union, so he and the producer who hired him thought everything was fine. But once Alex arrived on the set, a representative from ACTRA told him that he was prohibited from hosting the show because he wasn't a union member, and a Catch-22 situation quickly developed.

The show told Alex he would be sued for breach of contract if he refused to host the show, while the union informed him that he still couldn't work without becoming a member. Alex was stuck in the middle. The two sides went back and forth for a while, with neither ceding ground, until they hammered out an agreement at the last minute that allowed Alex to host the show for thirteen weeks without becoming a member of the union.

While he welcomed the work, the production company, Catalena Productions, was having money problems. Since the producer had gone to bat for him with the union, when he asked Alex if they could wait to pay him until the end of the quarter, he agreed, even though he wasn't thrilled with the arrangement.

After he received his first paycheck, the show was renewed for another thirteen weeks but was then was canceled. The production company cut him a check, but when he deposited it the bank informed him that there was no money in the account. After getting the runaround from the producer, Alex asked the union for help, and that's when the Catch-22 resumed: the union said it couldn't help because he wasn't a member.

Most of the cast and crew during that second thirteen-week period had had no idea that Catalena Productions was struggling financially—or that by the end of the show's run it had filed for bankruptcy. So when the bomb dropped, Alex wasn't the only one who got stiffed. He contacted a lawyer, who informed him that when it came to the list of staff and businesses to be paid once the company was liquidated, there was little chance he would ever see any money; carpenters and electricians were way ahead of him on the list, because toward the end of the second run they had gotten wind of the imminent bankruptcy and had filed mechanic's liens in advance so they could eventually get paid.

The money ran out long before the bankruptcy overseers reached Alex's place on the list. But he held on to the check as a reminder of the unpredictable nature of show business. Eventually, he framed it and hung it on his office wall.

"Paying one's dues," indeed.

Fortunately, his luck was about to change, at least in the professional realm.

In 1982 he received offers to film two separate pilots for new game shows. One was called *Malcolm*, and in it a cartoon character by that name shared cohosting duties with Alex and helped players come up with one word of a two-word answer. *Malcolm* was an example of a then-innovative animation technique called AniForm, where an offstage puppeteer operated the on-screen character and voiced the answers . . . and corny jokes. A few minutes' viewing is enough to understand why the pilot remained unsold.

The second pilot was for a game show called *Starcade*, which consisted of video-game players competing against one another on popular games of the day, from *Pac-Man* to *Donkey Kong*. An initial pilot had been shown on repeat in syndication for several weeks, and successful viewership numbers encouraged the producers to pursue it as a regular show. But they needed more episodes in order to sell the show, so Alex was brought in to tape three additional pilots.

During postproduction, he also pitched in to help edit the pilots he had filmed. It was a way to thank the producers for giving him a chance, but it also provided him with the opportunity to help out behind the scenes and actually have a hand in shaping a program, perhaps increasing the odds that a network would pick it up.

WTBS—Ted Turner's fledgling network—picked up the show in 1982, and the producers offered Alex the job. But he had to turn it down since by then he had gotten a job hosting *Battlestars*, a game show that was a variation on the then-popular celebrity show *Hollywood Squares*. Instead of nine celebrities sitting within the squares of a tic-tac-toe board offering up funny, often ribald answers to host Peter Marshall's questions, *Battlestars* featured six celebrities—the show's budget was a fraction of *Squares*', so it had to cut corners somewhere—sitting in triangles rather than in boxes.

The show was produced by Trebek's previous boss, Merrill Heatter, who had formed his own production company after his longtime partner, Bob Quigley, retired.

Alex was happy to be hosting a show again, especially with a producer he had worked with before, but he particularly loved the format and tone of *Battlestars*. "It was an ideal show, because I asked a question and the celebrity gave a funny answer," he said. "What a great way to make a living: you tell a joke and I laugh—give me a check, please."

The show lasted only six months before being canceled, and Heatter brought back a revamped version of the show a year later—*The New Battlestars*, again with Alex—but the overhaul wasn't enough to save it, and it was canceled after only thirteen weeks.

Around the same time, Alex was booked to host two other pilots. One was called *Love Me, Love Me Not* and was based on a successful game show in Italy called *M'ama Non M'ama*, where two men faced off against two women and took turns asking each other a series of romance-oriented questions. Next, Merrill Heatter wanted to bring back *High Rollers*, albeit slightly tweaked, and he hired Alex to tape two pilots for the new incarnation, *Lucky Numbers*. But neither show was picked up.

Of course, this was old hat to Alex. He dusted himself off and got busy looking for his next job.

Little did he know that the next job would be the one to stick.

FINALLY . . . *JEOPARDY!*

In 1963, Merv Griffin was looking for a new project.

Griffin, who had launched his career in show business as a singer with the 1949 radio hit "I've Got a Lovely Bunch of Coconuts"—for which he was paid the princely sum of 50 bucks—had succeeded by dabbling in a variety of areas, from working as an actor under contract to Warner Bros. with a few stints on Broadway thrown in, to hosting a TV game show called *Play Your Hunch*. A gig subbing on the *Jack Paar Show* in January 1962 proved to be so successful that he was hosting his own talk show before the end of the year.

The Merv Griffin Show was an instant hit, which critics attributed to his breezy rapport with guests of all stripes, as well as his insatiable curiosity. Merv's desire to learn a little about everything meant he was a dogged researcher. "I am a thick blotter of mostly useless information," he admitted.

The show lasted only two years before being canceled—it would be brought back in various incarnations over the years—but Merv was unperturbed; he committed to a season of acting in summer stock as well as filling in on a TV show called *Talent Scouts*. Most of all, he wanted to do another game show, not necessarily to host but to launch one from scratch. As a kid, he loved playing word games like Hangman with his sister during long car rides, but actually any game would do.

His new show, *Word for Word*, was about to debut in 1963, and as both producer and host he was running the show, which is what made him happiest. The show's concept revolved around anagrams, where contestants had to make as many small words as they could from one longer word.

He was thrilled to get the show on the air, since the contest-rigging game-show scandals of the late 1950s had soured networks and viewers on the format.

One day in 1963, Merv and his wife, Julann, were on a plane, trying to figure out how best to format the new show. When Julann suggested providing contestants with the answers, Merv reminded her that that was how game shows had ended up in hot water in the fifties.

Julann explained that, yes, the host would indeed be providing contestants with answers—but that the contestants would have to respond with questions!

Her husband gave her a confused look.

"The answer is '5,280,'" said Julann.

"How many feet in a mile?"

"The answer is '79 Wistful Vista.'"

"'Where did Fibber McGee and Molly live?'"

A lightbulb went off in Merv's head, and they spent the rest of the flight flinging answers and questions back and forth.

"By the time we landed," said Julann years later, "we had an idea for a show."

After Merv fleshed out the rules for the game, he approached a group of executives at NBC, who liked the idea and helped him to fine-tune the concept and format. In fact, they liked the idea so much that they didn't even order a pilot.

But their response to the name of the game—*What's the Question?*—was lukewarm. They also suggested that Griffin even out the tension in the game while raising the stakes. "They told me that in a show you can't have all hills," he later explained. "You've got to have valleys too, and something has to go wrong. Then they said, 'There are no jeopardies.'"

Another lightbulb—actually, this time closer to a lightning bolt. *There are no jeopardies.* The executives continued to hash out the details and arc of the game, but Griffin was no longer listening. "All I heard was 'jeopardy, jeopardy, jeopardy, jeopardy,' and that's how it got its name," he said.

Once the show was approved and had a name, Merv needed a theme song.

But just like the rules and format for his new show, the theme song had to swerve away from the typical music of the scandalized shows, which tended to favor the staccato sounds that newscasts employed. Merv needed a kinder, gentler snippet that would serve both for the music played at the beginning of the show and as the music played during the Final Jeopardy! round when contestants were trying to concentrate.

With all this swirling in his head, Merv sat down at his piano—one that actor Marlon Brando had given him several years before—and came up with the theme song in less than a minute.

Merv had also referred to the song as "A Time for Tony," a lullaby he had written when his son was an infant, but once the song was approved by NBC, he went ahead and wrote lyrics that applied specifically to the game:

> *We're in trouble, yes indeed,*
> *We are all in Jeopardy!*

Next it was time to find a host.

Merv and NBC interviewed a number of actors. He had spotted Art Fleming, a patrician type of actor who had appeared in numerous films and on TV series, and who at the time was working as the main anchor of the eleven o'clock news on New York's NBC station and appearing in commercials for local businesses on the side. Merv thought he had makings of a successful game-show host, and after a brief audition, Fleming got the job on the side.

Jeopardy! debuted on March 30, 1964, and soon developed a loyal and diverse audience, from college students watching during their lunch break to young housewives and mothers who welcomed the intellectual challenge. Reports of blue-collar workers like plumbers and taxi drivers tucking into diners to watch on their breaks were also widespread.

In addition to the challenge, viewers especially liked the show for its unchanging format; they always knew exactly what to expect. The show happily chugged along for more than a decade before cracks started to appear in its façade.

When *Jeopardy!* first appeared in 1964, the United States had enjoyed a comfortable and prosperous postwar period during which sociological roles and economic growth were givens. But a decade later, after the psychedelic era of the late 1960s, protests against the Vietnam War, and widespread sociological upheaval, the country looked very different indeed, and some network executives were chomping at the bit to make sure that TV programming reflected the societal changes and attracted younger viewers.

Jeopardy! aired at lunchtime in most of the markets across the country. But when NBC hired Lin Bolen as the new head of daytime programming, she launched a slash-and-burn assault that would help bring the network more up-to-date.

First she moved *Jeopardy!* to an earlier time slot, forcing most college-aged viewers to abandon ship. Then she reversed course and moved the show to the afternoon, where it faced off against *Let's Make a Deal* and *As the World Turns*, both popular shows that *Jeopardy!* couldn't compete against. The show's cancellation quickly followed.

It was a not-so-open secret that Bolen pulled these moves because she wanted Art Fleming gone—her mission was to attract younger viewers to the network—and she knew that Merv would never fire him.

Merv was disappointed when the show ended in 1975, but Bolen and the network placated him by buying *Wheel of Fortune*—the Hangman-themed show he had developed—and launching it just days after *Jeopardy!* went off the air.

• • •

Jeopardy! got a second chance in late 1978 when NBC brought it back from the dead as *The All-New Jeopardy!*, with Art Fleming again serving as host, despite Lin Bolen's objections. *Wheel of Fortune* had proven to be a big success for the network, so this time Merv had the upper hand.

The show was tweaked slightly—a fourth round called Super Jeopardy! was added—and Merv moved production from New York to Los Angeles. But the updated version didn't attract many returning viewers—or new viewers, for that matter—and the show was canceled after only five months because of low ratings.

This time, Merv accepted full blame for the failure. "The original *Jeopardy!* had a far more loyal audience than even I realized, and they didn't like anyone messing with its basic structure," he said.

He filed that lesson away for the future, vowing that *Jeopardy!* would get another shot at success. In the meantime, he returned his focus to making sure *Wheel* continued to be a success.

His chance came sooner than he thought.

A certain board game called Trivial Pursuit took a while to catch on when it was first introduced in 1981, but once it did take off, people of all intellectual stripes latched onto the game as a way to test and compare their knowledge against others. By 1984, the game had sold twenty million sets.

Merv had clearly noticed the phenomenon, and he decided that the success of the board game proved it was clearly time to give his beloved *Jeopardy!* another try. King World

Productions had bought the syndication rights to *Wheel of Fortune* from Merv and wanted to pair it with another show, figuring stations would find a package of game shows more appealing than just one. *Jeopardy!* was the natural choice.

But some station executives and programmers were against reincarnating *Jeopardy!* for a second time, especially at night; after all, it was the era of game shows like *Hollywood Squares*, and *The Price Is Right*, and *Match Game*. These naysayers said that *Jeopardy!* was still too difficult, and that audiences preferred their game shows to have celebrities cracking off-color jokes or people jumping up and down, screaming, and kissing the host, not a trio of eggheads standing stiffly behind their podiums, faces flushed and sweaty, chewing their lips as they racked their brains searching for the right answer to Final Jeopardy!

But one advantage was that the show came with a built-in audience. "[People] tell me how they used to play hooky or call in sick to see the show," said Mark Richards, a contestant coordinator for the show. "These people were, for the most part, teenagers when *Jeopardy!* was first on. Now they're in their thirties and forties and they still remember the show." When the *Jeopardy!* pilot aired at a convention for the National Association of Television Program Executives, stations in 130 different markets signed up, with some claiming it was "the fastest-selling syndicated show" to date.

There was, however, a bit of tinkering with the basic premise of the show's successful run under Art Fleming. Unlike the earlier incarnation, players who came in second and third place weren't allowed to go home with the money they had won. Producers observed that many contestants had essentially stopped wagering after they reached a specific figure—say, enough for a down payment on a house or a long-awaited vacation. This had obviously cut down on the suspense of the game and the amount of money that was bet during the Final Jeopardy! round.

Griffin also heeded Lin Bolen's advice to relaunch the show with a new, younger host who could attract audiences both young and old. Alex was the natural choice.

He didn't have to audition, because he had developed quite a track record since arriving in the States over a decade earlier. But more important, they knew he could more than hold his own. Back in August 1980, when he was between gigs and his marriage was falling apart, Alex had stepped in on very short notice to substitute for regular *Wheel of Fortune* host Chuck Woolery.

It turned out that Woolery—who had hosted the show since it first aired in 1975—was distraught after his wife, actress Jo Ann Pflug, had announced she was leaving him. He attempted suicide and landed in the hospital, and was in no shape to host the show.

Normally, taping would have been postponed, but that particular week it wasn't an option, since the show was running a special tournament and many of the contestants had already flown in from across the country. The producers ran through a list of possible hosts, and the only one they all agreed was good enough to effortlessly slip into the role was Alex.

Woolery returned to work when he got out of the hospital, and he and Pflug would eventually divorce. Around the same time, Woolery tried to negotiate a salary increase, and after turning down an initial offer from Griffin, he dug in his heels and went on strike. So Merv—a notorious penny-pincher—fired him.

And that's how Pat Sajak—who was working as a weatherman on a local Los Angeles TV station at the time—came to host *Wheel of Fortune.*

But Alex had also been on the radar of one of Merv's good friends, the beloved comedienne Lucille Ball. One day, Merv mentioned to Ball that he was resurrecting *Jeopardy!* She had been a big fan of *High Rollers,* and told Merv he ought to take a look at Alex.

When producer Bob Murphy called him with the offer, Alex was thrilled at the prospect of hosting again, but after getting stiffed on *Pitfall,* he wanted to make sure he wouldn't be working for free. So he asked Murphy if he was planning to pay him.

Of course, Murphy replied, and named a figure.

Alex was well aware of Merv's reputation for cheapness, but he was still caught off guard: the salary was 50 percent less than what he was paid on *Battlestars.*

But he wanted to work, so he asked if he could also serve as a producer on the show and earn an extra salary for the job. Murphy—and Merv—agreed, and Alex had a job again, with a salary that came close to that of his previous job.

He was back.

The show debuted on September 10, 1984.

"We came on the air very quietly, without any great fanfare," said Alex. "There were no fireworks, no bright lights, no wild and crazy music."

Jeopardy! was well received, but of course Trebek never believed it was a sure thing; after all, his longest tenure as a game-show host up to that point was two years. Since game shows were not known for their longevity, both Alex and the producers had their doubts as to whether the show would still be on the air a year later. Besides, from the beginning of the relaunch, station managers across the country were complaining to King World that the questions and answers on the show were too difficult, ones that stumped the average viewer. They asked King World if the writers could dumb down the questions, and Alex and the other producers said they would.

A few months later, the same stations that had complained were now getting in touch to thank the producers for making the questions easier, but Alex and the producers just laughed, because they hadn't asked the writers to simplify the show; instead, the various station executives only *thought* they would be easier, and so that's what they chose to see.

The staff defended both their show's format and dignity. "This is not *Beat the Clock*," said David Williger, an executive producer of the show. "We do not give our winners a year's supply of macaroni."

For his part, Alex was thrilled to be back in the game. "I was happy to be working, and I was having a good time," he said. "Because I was producing, I was making decisions that affected how the game would play, and that pleased me to no end." His production duties ranged from developing variations on the game—the first Tournament of Champions aired in the fall of 1985, with fifteen winners from the first year facing off against one another for $100,000—to putting his home-improvement skills to the test by making sure that every lightbulb in the studio was working.

After eleven years of uncertainty and change—sometimes with only a moment's notice that he was out of work yet again—Alex was gratified that it looked like *Jeopardy!* would be around for a while. After just one year, the show was the number two syndicated game show in the country, just after *Wheel of Fortune.* Alex loved helping to produce the show, and was thinking of branching out into other roles in the entertainment industry, since he didn't want to be viewed as just a game-show host. "Rarely does anyone in show business take us seriously, even though we do well in a difficult job," he said.

Based on his days at the CBC, he knew he was capable of juggling a variety of responsibilities, and so much the better if they provided him with opportunities where he could learn new things and challenge his brain. But he was already starting to see how the entertainment business in the States and Hollywood put—and kept—its stars in neat little boxes, for marketing purposes but also to keep them easy to handle. e.g., you're a game-show host, not an actor. The CBC had never placed such restrictions upon him, in fact, quite the opposite.

Alex bristled against the constraints, but his production work on the show helped ease his concerns and gave him hope that he had the skills—and would have the opportunities—to become known as more than simply a game-show host. "Producing *Jeopardy!* for the last three years has whetted my appetite," he said.

"I don't want to be a game-show host forever."

But it looked like he'd be able to stay at the helm of the show for as long as he wanted. In December 1986, a few local ABC stations started to bump their half-hour national news broadcasts to earlier time slots, in part because ratings for *Jeopardy!* were so good. In New York, executives at WABC-TV shifted the network's *World News Tonight with Peter Jennings* to 6:30 while *Jeopardy!* took over the seven o'clock slot, figuring that if viewers could get their news a half hour earlier—with no other network news broadcasts to compete against at that time—then *Jeopardy!* would go up against the *CBS Evening News with Dan Rather* and the *Nightly News with Tom Brokaw* on NBC. In other words, viewers could get caught up on the news thirty minutes early before settling in for an enjoyable and intellectually challenging half hour of *Jeopardy!* and Alex Trebek.

Producers and anchors on the news shows at all three networks weren't thrilled with the changes, and there was at least one group of die-hard fans that was unhappy with the new starting time. Davey Johnson, manager of the New York Mets, lobbied WABC to shift the show even earlier, complaining that at some games only a few players showed up on the field for the National Anthem before the start of games at 7:30 because they were glued to the TV during Final Jeopardy!

Other major markets soon picked up the same schedule, but Merv decided to reverse the order of his two game shows, running *Wheel of Fortune* at 7, followed by *Jeopardy!* at 7:30. The combination soon became known as the "golden hour," and turned into a no-brainer for local stations desperate for increased revenue at a time when the recession of the late 1980s—spurred by a 1987 stock market crash known as Black

Monday—took root and showed no signs of yielding anytime soon.

Viewers needed their nightly fixes of answers offered up in the form of a question—as well as some security during a turbulent economic period—and the audience for *Jeopardy!* continued to increase. Alex took this as a sign of job security, and decided that he could finally put down roots.

So in his time away from the *Jeopardy!* set, he designed and helped to build his own house on a two-acre lot high above Mulholland Drive. The 5,500-square-foot home had a modern sensibility, with white walls, nineteen-foot-high ceilings, large open-concept rooms—including four bedrooms—and several terraces and outside decks to take advantage of the stellar view of the San Fernando Valley. While the house had a deliberately stark feel, Alex decorated the rooms with Asian art, wooden African sculptures, and a variety of antiques that helped warm it up.

Something else would have warmed up the house as well—a girlfriend—but Alex still seemed a bit spooked after the demise of his marriage. In public, however, he blamed his single state on his workaholic tendencies. "I don't have enough time to devote to a relationship," he said.

Though he continued to date, no woman had yet won his heart. Ruta Lee, his old sidekick on *High Rollers*, had tried to set him up with female celebrities, including actress Stefanie Powers and TV gossip columnist Rona Barrett, but nothing ever stuck. "What his friends think is right for Alex is never what Alex thinks is right for Alex," said Lee.

But once the house was completed in 1986, a woman *did*

move into Alex's new digs: his mother, Lucille. Not only did Alex welcome the company in the huge, sprawling house, but Lucille immediately assumed some of his household duties, running errands and doing the food shopping, though he still did much of the cooking, gourmet and ideally for ten guests, no more and no fewer. She also helped out with some projects around the house, including the new in-ground swimming pool, for which she helped her son set up plywood frames in which to pour the concrete.

Several four-legged friends also moved in, including two cats that Alex rescued from the local animal shelter: a male Russian Blue mix named Winger Dinger and a female Persian mix named Sleaze Bucket, or Sleazy for short. At one time, he also had a cat named Safety Puce. "I don't like ordinary names; I want something with personality," he said. "It's my weird sense of humor."

He also had dogs, including a collie mix named Jake, but he had to be careful about letting them outside since his neighborhood contained a variety of predatory wildlife, including owls and coyotes. Spammer was a Yorkshire-Pomeranian mix whom Alex loved, but one day a coyote got him.

While Alex had always been fond of animals, he had issues with pet lovers who had no empathy for humans who were suffering just as badly as—or worse than—the animals they doted on. "It's fine to care for animals, but show some concern for human suffering," he said.

As he surrounded himself with his beloved pets, Lucille still wanted her son to add a woman to his life. "The longer he stays single, the harder it's going to be," she said. "He's become so self-sufficient."

He had indeed gone back into his shell. When a clue on a 1987 *Jeopardy!* show referred to flamingos and their mating habits—just once a year was necessary, it turned out—Alex nodded in commiseration even though it had been years since his divorce. "Flamingos and I have a great deal in common," he commented, perhaps giving away more information than he had intended.

With his visibility on the increase, Alex branched out by joining a fledgling at-home shopping program known as Value Television, aka VTV, in January 1986. He teamed up with actress Meredith MacRae to host a one-hour home shopping show.

In an era when Americans did their shopping by mail by paging through thick catalogs—the Sears, Roebuck catalog was still a mainstay of American consumer life, particularly the Christmas edition—doing your shopping by watching a show and picking up the phone to order was unheard-of when Home Shopping Network, today known as HSN, pioneered the concept by launching a bare-bones program on a local cable channel in Florida in 1982. The format proved to be so successful that the channel went national in 1985. A major competitor, QVC—short for Quality Value Convenience— debuted on June 13, 1986, and a year later had pulled in more than $112 million.

VTV was launched by Hanover House, a national company producing twenty-four mail-order catalogs catering to a variety of niche audiences, from housewives to gay men via International Male. While VTV started as a one-hour show, the company expected to quickly expand as consumers became more comfortable with the idea of shopping via their TVs. The show focused on selling the more than twenty-five thousand products offered in the company's catalogs one at a time, from corkscrews to phone answering machines. Popular TV stars of the day would come on board for an interview segment with Alex and Meredith to exchange witty banter, and with any luck encourage viewers to pick up their phones and place an order.

On the show, Alex appears animated and engaged when talking with guests like Ken Kercheval of *Dallas* fame and explaining the various items featured on the program. Based on the success of competitors HSN and QVC, Alex believed he had signed on with a shooting star. "I felt it would work because it mixed products with talk," he said.

But his career as a shopping channel host turned out to be short-lived; after a promising start, the ratings started to tank, and the producers decided the best way to stem the bleeding was to ramp up the hard sell. Alex balked at the new approach, and he left after just thirteen weeks; he was replaced by hyperactive fitness star Richard Simmons.

It was good riddance as far as he was concerned, and he later referred to the endless parade of corn poppers and frying pans as "crap."

But he wasn't at all crushed. Conversely, his dismissal from VTV meant that he had time to scope out more opportunities, as well as to volunteer his services and donate money to nonprofits and organizations that helped people around the world as well as in his own neighborhood. "Like most people who have achieved a certain degree of success in life, it behooves you to start giving back," he affirmed.

Alex also participated in charity sporting events, though sometimes there were physical repercussions. During a celebrity softball game, he slid into home and wrecked his knee, tearing the cartilage and severing a ligament.

In 1985 he became involved with World Vision, a nonprofit organization that helps bring relief efforts to people living in impoverished countries around the world. He pegged his desire to help to the famine in Ethiopia that started to appear in news reports in 1984. "I just looked at these children and thought, 'I've got to do something,'" he said.

"I wanted to do more than just send in a contribution," he said, explaining that he had no qualms about taking advantage of his celebrity status to help people in dire need. So he got in touch with a friend who was involved with World Vision, and together they came up with the idea of Alex going on location to various projects sponsored by the group and reporting feature stories about the projects from those areas.

On his first assignment, he visited an orphanage in Thailand, and what he saw affected him deeply. A toddler approached him and gestured to Alex that he wanted to be picked up. Alex cradled the boy in his arms, but when he set him back down on the ground the boy began to wail piteously. A nurse nearby told him, "It's tough for them, because they get so little human compassion or physical warmth that they don't want to let go."

On another day, he was helping to distribute food to families who lived nearby when a woman rushed up to him and pushed her clearly malnourished baby into his arms, asking him to adopt the child. "It was heartbreaking stuff," he admitted.

That first visit made an indelible impression on him, and he vowed to help whenever and wherever he could. On Christmas Eve in 1989, he helped serve dinner to the homeless community at the Los Angeles Mission, dishing out baked ham, sweet potatoes, and pumpkin pie to more than five thousand men, women, and children in one day alongside actors Laraine Newman, Mike Farrell, and Katherine Helmond.

"We shouldn't have this problem in this rich country," he said.

6

SETTLING IN

In 1987, Alex was relieved of his producer responsibilities after spending three years producing the show. He had mixed feelings about his freed-up schedule.

"I'm a problem solver," he said. "It gives me satisfaction. I don't like running away from challenges." On the other hand, he conceded that his schedule was so consuming that he had no life outside of work. "I'd become a terrible workaholic—[some days] you'd have to send me home in a Baggie."

So now, with some of the pressure off, he had more time to pursue other experiences. For a while, he studied everything he could about bullfighting, reading books and watching movies and then traveling to Spain to witness the actual event. "I came home with two capes and a sword," he said. After eighteen months, he switched gears and plunged into an in-depth study of Nazi Germany, which was then followed by the Civil War.

Some days he was tempted to chuck it all and leave *Jeopardy!* for a year or so, but he realized that if he did drop out for a while it would be difficult to return to his old life, both personally and career-wise. "I could see myself in some far-off land for a year working distributing food, helping in relief," he said. "But I'd be replaced, and it's tough to get back in."

So he stayed put, never losing sight of the advantages of having a job with a schedule that allowed him to work two days every two weeks. Besides, the popularity of the show just continued to grow. Three years after *Jeopardy!* launched, the number of stations airing the show had increased by 10 percent. His job was secure, enabling him to pursue some very eclectic opportunities, including guest-starring in a 1988 episode of *Mama's Family*, a sitcom spinoff from *The Carol Burnett Show* to showcase actress Vicki Lawrence's "Mama" character. Alex and Vicki were dating at the time, and when she invited him on the show, he jumped at the chance.

But instead of playing a role that would call on him to summon his acting chops, the script cast him as himself in the role of *Jeopardy!* host. The episode aired in February 1988 and featured Mama winning a spot on the show after acing the audition.

Alex also made a guest appearance on an episode of the hit sitcom *Cheers* that aired on January 18, 1990, in which he again played himself. After he showed up for the first table-read rehearsal, the writers were so impressed with his delivery that they revamped the script to give him a bigger role. "They had discovered that I could handle lines, and so each day they added a few," he said.

Though his on-screen time amounted to only a few minutes, it made an indelible impression on fans, who often cited his appearance when meeting Alex in person. "People still ask me about that," he said.

Mailman Cliff Clavin, played by actor John Ratzenberger, was the resident trivia expert at the Boston bar on *Cheers*. The premise of the episode—entitled "What Is . . . Cliff Clavin?"—was that *Jeopardy!* taped a week of shows in Boston, and Cliff auditioned and won a spot as a contestant. He amassed $22,000 before the Final Jeopardy! round, which featured an answer in a film category about three movie stars. Cliff was totally stuck, so he wrote, "Who are three people who've never been in my kitchen?"

Alex headed to the bar after the show where he ran into Cliff. He told Cliff that his answer was a valid one and that he was now questioning his role on the show. "How can I go on hosting the program if I'm filled with all these doubts?" He later disclosed to bar regular Norm Peterson—played by George Wendt—that he was only kidding and that he'd made up the story because Cliff made him uneasy.

Alex had a blast on the show, and would rack up appearances in movies including *Rain Man* and *White Men Can't Jump*, and on the TV programs *The Golden Girls* and *The Larry Sanders Show*. He played himself as *Jeopardy!* host in every one, but he clearly aspired for more.

In 1989, Alex received his first Daytime Emmy Award for Outstanding Game Show Host. Some felt it was long overdue, but he was as humble as ever and greatly honored by the win.

As viewership and the number of stations continued to increase, he was a bit hesitant about the unbridled growth.

In fact, in 1989 he took great issue with a Boston station that aired episodes at 7:30 P.M. and rebroadcast them at 11:30 P.M., even complaining to station executives. "I don't want to see it on the air that much," he said. "If you've got something good, look after it, nurture it. I love chocolate brownies, but if I ate forty of them, that fortieth one would go down very slowly."

Former host Art Fleming also weighed in on the show's success. He was generally complimentary about how Alex had been handling the game, but still perhaps a bit stung from being put out to pasture, so he had a few choice words about the new version. While he believed it was far superior to other game shows of the day, he thought the clues were actually easier than when he had presided over the show. In addition, he said that the pace of the game had slowed considerably, and he dismissed the policy of only the winning contestant keeping the prize money. "That's a little chintzy for me," he said.

"In my day, runners-up used to get to keep their prize money. Now they get a carton of dog food or something! You finish a dollar out of first place and you win a year's supply of lip gloss!"

But Merv Griffin—who of course was laughing all the way to the bank—thought the show was a vast improvement over Fleming's version, particularly when it came to the quality of the contestants, who back in the 1960s tended toward "heavy intellectuals and earth mamas we pulled out of bookstores," said Griffin. "None of them seemed too concerned with grooming. I was very nervous about it."

However, there were some critics who didn't think the contestants had changed all that much from the Art Fleming days. One reviewer of a show from early in Trebek's reign opined that they "bear an uncomfortable resemblance to people you'd see in a supermarket carefully pricing Campbell's Soup for One."

Alex, for his part, just kept plowing ahead, the advice from his former producer never to turn down a job still ringing in his ears. In addition to his work on *Jeopardy!*, in 1987 Alex took on hosting duties for *Classic Concentration*, another reboot of a game show. To win prizes, contestants had to uncover and match cards on top of a rebus puzzle that slowly revealed itself as more cards were matched.

In a way, it was the polar opposite of *Jeopardy!*, and Alex classified the differences between the two shows as a matter of timing: on *Concentration*, the pace was looser, and he spent more time chatting with contestants and making idle conversation, because a contestant's fate was not dictated by the clock. *Jeopardy!*, by contrast, had always been fast-paced, Fleming's critique notwithstanding. Alex was acutely aware of the influence that time had on the game, since if one contestant had a big lead, the others would want the chance to come from behind, which idle conversation would interfere with. "I'm [not] going to waste fifteen seconds by telling a joke," he said.

One night in 1988, Alex headed off to a dinner party at the home of his friend Bud Krause, a past president of the automotive chain Pep Boys. Jean Currivan, a twenty-five-year-old project manager at a property development firm in Los Angeles, was at the same dinner.

At that point, Alex had been alone for almost a decade. He

was still pretty pessimistic about his chances for building—and keeping—a long-term relationship. Earlier that year on the show, Peggy Kennedy, one of the contestants on the Seniors Tournament, had told Alex during the getting-to-know-you contestant chat on the show that she was a forensic toxicologist, and only worked with dead bodies. "We won't have anything to do with you when you're alive," she quipped. After the laughter died down, Alex shot back, "You're not the first woman to have said that, believe me!"

Jean didn't fit into his typical category of eligible women, since he mostly dated women who were his age or even a little bit older.

But Jean had intrigued him when they'd met at a party a year earlier, where Alex "thought she was most attractive and she thought I was a jerk." Unbeknownst to her, Alex had secretly set up their second meeting by telling Krause that he would attend the party if he also invited Jean.

At the second dinner, they reconnected, and this time Jean didn't turn away. To Alex, she was a breath of fresh air. Some onlookers at the dinner party described their meeting as love at first sight, though Jean denied it. However, she may have viewed their second meeting as an omen.

"Her mother [later] told me that when Jean was growing up, she'd be playing house and she'd be waiting for her husband Alex to come home," he said. "That's kind of spooky."

Alex asked her to dinner at his house, and she accepted, though she tried not to show that she was anxious about dating the famous star of a beloved game show. "I was afraid I'd mispronounce my own name!" she admitted. "But Alex is really down-to-earth; he's much more casual than he is on the show."

Jean grew up in Huntington, New York, a town on Long Island about thirty-five miles from midtown Manhattan, and was something of an anomaly among the women in Hollywood, many of who had Alex in their crosshairs. For one thing, although she had done some modeling, she openly admitted that she wasn't a fan of glamour or of wearing makeup. But more important, she didn't like to have the spotlight on her; with a brother who was often sick and a younger sister who looked up to her—and parents who expected her to fill their roles—Jean had served as the caretaker for her entire family during her childhood, and it was a role she was comfortable with. "Having to focus on me is a challenge," she admitted.

Though she acknowledged that her childhood was tough, there were also clear benefits. "It showed me the depths of my compassion, the fortitude of my character, and the grace with which I could confront any challenging situation," she said.

After graduating from Harborfields High School in Greenlawn, New York, in 1982, Jean headed to California, where she studied business administration and took a job at a property management firm. She had been in California for six years when she and Alex started dating.

They were soon inseparable. Alex particularly liked the fact that they shared similar values. But he also realized that he had grown up, and that what he wanted in a woman had changed. "Maturing has taught me that I need a supportive woman," he admitted. "I can be—and am—constantly in charge. But it's nice to come home and let someone else do the nurturing."

Jean clearly fit the bill, and she was attracted to him as well. "There was just this deep sensitivity about him, with a gruffy exterior," she said.

Happily, his friends clearly approved of Jean. "Alex always had great taste, whether in music, books, crystal, or wives," said Alan Thicke.

"Alex was looking for a Jean," said Bob Murphy, executive producer of *Jeopardy!* "And he found her."

"She's more beautiful inside than she is outside," said Alex, "and she has a charitable nature that endears her to everybody she meets. I feel very good when I'm with her, and I feel terrible when we're apart."

Their twenty-four-year age difference caused some concern for both of them. "At first it worried me," he said, "but then I thought, 'The hell with it. We'll make it work.'"

"I can understand why he was cautious about being with a younger woman," said Jean, "so I didn't try to push him. We just took it one day at a time."

But it quickly became apparent that the difference in their ages was not important, and after they had been dating a year, Alex decided to pop the question, on Jean's twenty-sixth birthday.

He already had some definite ideas of the right and wrong way to go about it. In a slightly tongue-in-cheek article in *Men's Health* magazine, Alex doled out some advice on how to propose marriage based on his years of experience hosting *Jeopardy!*: "If she's the right answer, what is the question? If it's 'Who is the last woman I'll ever make love to?' and you're fine with the answer, great," he said. "But if your question is 'Who is a convenient solution to my bachelorhood problem?' then don't ring in just yet."

He handed her a gift-wrapped box that contained a pair of black velvet pants and a matching bolero jacket. "I thought that was it," she said, but then Alex pulled out a small wicker box. "Here's a little something else," he said with a smile. She opened the box to find a sapphire-and-diamond ring. Jean was speechless, and then he dropped to one knee.

He went public with his engagement on Dinah Shore's afternoon talk show, *A Conversation with Dinah.* "I'm going to be married, and this is the first time I've said it out loud," he said, his nerves apparent.

While many couples share a favorite song, Alex and Jean quickly discovered that it was instead a movie that symbolized their love: *Wuthering Heights.* "We feel the same powerful kind of love Heathcliff and Cathy felt," he said.

To celebrate their engagement, the couple traveled to Yorkshire, England, where the story was set, and replicated the journey of the characters. They wandered through the moors and hiked to a dilapidated stone farmhouse that supposedly served as the inspiration for Emily Brontë's dark, brooding novel. They stood before the ruins for a while, reveling in the history and the stunning view of the valley.

A line from the movie popped into his head. "'Whatever our souls are made of, yours and mine are the same,'" he said. "That's the way Jeannie and I think of ourselves." They were heading back down the trail when torrential rains swept through, and they ran toward an old stable and etched their names into the stone, their love forever captured for posterity.

After they returned to California, they began to plan the wedding. But there was trouble looming.

Alex had always regarded the ups and downs of the business as part of the overall deal, saying that whenever he made a mistake on the show, whether an incorrect pronunciation or the wrong question for a clue, the response was instantaneous, in the form of mail and phone calls from incensed viewers. "People have to channel their frustrations, their anger, so they look for likely targets, like me," he said. "It's a way to vent their own frustrations without anyone being able to take recourse against them. The tension comes with the territory. That's why I'm paid big bucks."

He usually tried to take the uproar in stride. "Celebrities are fair game," he said. "We're targets for all kinds of abuse, but you can't let it bother you too much."

For the most part, the relationship between Alex and his millions of fans was cordial, and sometimes downright friendly, as in the handwritten notes he often sent to fans who had just written in to request a glossy photo, probably expecting no more than a black-and-white headshot with a rubber-stamped autograph.

They were also inclined to latch onto the tiniest of his on-air comments and to respond with gifts. For instance, once he mentioned that he liked to collect baseball caps, and within a week they started to arrive in droves from all over the country, sent by fans who thrilled at the thought of Alex Trebek wearing *their* cap. Soon over five hundred of them—

printed with everything from "I Survived Skylab" to tiny oil derricks—had flooded his office.

To make room, he donated a couple hundred of them to a local charity, but they still arrived by the binful for several months after he made his announcement. He later joked that instead of mentioning that he liked baseball caps, he should have aimed a little higher and said that he liked to stockpile Rolex watches.

Indeed, though he was a relentless hoarder and never liked to throw anything out, Jean said that it wasn't easy to buy presents for her husband-to-be, because Alex was a very straightforward man and didn't care for anything with a designer label or that was in any way impractical. Besides, if he wanted something, he was more than happy to get it himself. When he said to Jean one day that he'd love to be able to play a musical instrument, she bought him a guitar along with a package of lessons. He accepted the gift, but picked up the instrument only a couple of times before giving it away.

Through the years, he'd shrugged off unwanted intrusions, like the woman who showed up at a book signing and handed him a cupcake topped with breasts made out of frosting, and the female fans—mostly in their sixties and seventies—who appeared at public events and begged him to grow his mustache back. He also hosted the Pillsbury Bake-Off for several years, and one year a contestant was overheard asking the judges, "Is Alex here yet, and do you know his room number?"

But once word got out about their pending nuptials, attention grew as reporters from several of the more unsavory supermarket tabloids started to swarm.

Although admittedly, Alex didn't live the kind of lifestyle that would regularly get his name splashed across the front pages of *Star* magazine and the *National Enquirer*, his wedding apparently fell into a different category. As a result, Alex later reported that the *National Enquirer* told him that unless he gave them the exclusive rights to cover the wedding, they'd send several helicopters to hover over the event, which enraged him. When he refused, the *National Enquirer* printed an article saying that Jean was pregnant at the time of their wedding, to retaliate.

Around the same time, a woman had been stalking him and Jean for at least two years, since their relationship was made public; she'd been calling him regularly at home and sending threatening letters. One day when she called, Jean answered the phone, taped their exchange, and contacted the police, who were able to track the woman down. Alex suspected that she was the source who had called the *Enquirer* with the fake story about Jean's pregnancy.

"It was an out-and-out lie," said Alex. "My wife was upset, and my mother, a traditionalist, was angry."

But when April 30, 1990, arrived, they put everything aside to focus on their happiness. Alex and Jean were married at the Regency Club in Los Angeles, with 150 friends and relatives attending. Trebek responded to the critical question by saying, "The answer is . . . yes."

The *National Enquirer* finally printed a retraction to its story on November 5, 1990, more than six months after the wedding. "But the situation took its toll on me," Alex admitted.

Though he was clearly annoyed at the unwanted intrusions, he remained remarkably sanguine about the situation, and to put things in perspective he turned to the lessons he had learned as a philosophy major back in college. "I'm interested in why people are the way they are and why they do the things they do," he said.

Though there's a long history of mothers-in-law not getting along with their sons' new wives, happily a strong bond had developed between Alex's mom, Lucille, and Jean shortly after they began dating. "They get along like a house on fire," said Alex, almost to the point where he occasionally felt like a third wheel.

"Lucille's great," said Jean. "She has her own friends and does her own thing. And she's there for me in the evenings if Alex isn't home."

Though Alex and Jean went from the dinner party to wedding in just eighteen months, he said that it was impossible to think of living without her. "If I had not met her, I would have become very self-centered and set in my ways," he said.

Alex was determined to make things right the second time around. "In my first marriage I was ill-prepared, and I made a lot of mistakes," he admitted. "This time, I know what's expected of me; I won't make the same mistakes. If you don't know what's expected, how can you do the right thing?"

He immediately started to apply one very important lesson. "I learned from my first marriage that having more than one mistress of the house is not ideal," he said. "Though Jean and my mother are great buddies, it's best that each has a home to call her own." And so shortly after their wedding, Alex made plans to build a new house for himself and Jean, while constructing a separate guest house on the property where Lucille could live.

He bought thirty-five acres in the Hollywood Hills for $1.5 million, and planned to put their dream house at the very top of the mountain.

Though Alex had been steeped in the Catholic faith as a boy, he viewed religion to be largely a private affair. And he regarded spirituality—as separate from a particular Christian denomination—as largely out there in the realm of New Age types and the like.

But he did once admit to believing in a spiritual force outside of traditional religion, owing to an event that occurred one day while he was strolling the streets of New York City in the late 1970s.

Whenever he was assigned to host a new game show—and occasionally when *Jeopardy!* began to air in a new market—Alex would travel around the country on publicity excursions, during which he'd appear on TV and radio programs and talk up the show to newspaper reporters. He frequently traveled to New York on these trips, and when he wasn't in meetings he'd spend hours wandering around the city.

He liked to visit the usual attractions: museums like the Guggenheim and the Museum of Modern Art, as well as the Statue of Liberty and Central Park. One day he was walking up Fifth Avenue on the east side of the park, and suddenly something compelled him to stop in front of a mansion at the corner of 79th Street.

"Something got me—not intellectually, but at a gut

level—with this particular house," he said, thinking that if he ever moved to Manhattan, he'd move into this building.

He stepped toward the building to get a closer look, and saw a sign that read "Ukrainian Institute of America."

He was awestruck, and for a moment he was unable to move. "There is a power up there that influences us in ways we never know about," he said.

While he was stunned by the experience, he typically played it down, painting his wife as far more spiritual than he. "I'm more of a fatalist," he explained. "I deal with the realities, and I try to cope as best as I can with what's going on as it is happening."

He also said he preferred to look outside of himself for inspiration and meaning—particularly regarding the benefits of his job—than to look inside, maintaining that his visibility as the host of *Jeopardy!* allowed him to have countless experiences that he wouldn't have otherwise had. "It has provided me with opportunities to explore the world geographically, socially, and philanthropically," he said. "Doing that has allowed me to develop as a human."

Despite his pragmatic attitude, the geographic majesty that he encountered in the world has never failed to amaze him. "If you can't be in awe of Mother Nature," he said, "then there's something wrong with you."

In 1990, Alex could hardly believe his good fortune. He had long ago given up on finding someone to share his life, but now he had it all: a successful career, a wife he cherished, and plenty of time to enjoy it all.

And there was even more to come.

7

FINDING FAMILY

As the 1990s began, Alex was running on all cylinders.

In 1990, an average of fifteen million people were watching *Jeopardy!* every night, and the show was airing on 191 stations around the country. In fact, *Jeopardy!* was second only to *Wheel of Fortune* in terms of the number of viewers and syndicated stations on which it appeared. In addition, over a quarter of a million people took the test for a chance to compete on the show.

Alex wasn't the least bit surprised at the popularity and longevity of the show. "People like *Jeopardy!* because it's a good show and because it's tough," he said. "The viewers are competitive and they want to compete against the contestants themselves. We want to aspire to the better things in life, even though we may watch *The Gong Show* on a regular basis."

While many viewers and critics hailed the show as a pleasant, fast-paced way for viewers to challenge themselves, others had a different take on its popularity.

"*Jeopardy!* is a very classic hero's journey," said Bob Harris, author of *Prisoner of Trebekistan*, in which he detailed his experience on the show after winning five games in 1997 and competing in several tournaments. "The contestant is achieving goals with escalating stakes and obstacles. There's even a three-act structure."

With a new wife and a dream house to design and help build, Alex had enough on his plate. Plus, he and Jean had recently learned that she would give birth to their first child in February 1991. They were understandably overjoyed, as well as incredibly nervous. But those words—"Never turn down a job"—were still front and center in his mind.

He had signed on with the game show *Classic Concentration* back in 1987, and had found juggling the two shows to be relatively effortless. So when NBC approached him to host *To Tell the Truth* after retired football star Lynn Swann had to pull out due to scheduling conflicts, Alex readily agreed to step in. As a result, he became the first game-show host in history to juggle three different shows simultaneously.

While he might have taken on a fourth if it had been offered to him, Alex did have his own personal limits when it came to the type of show he would agree to host. "I'm sometimes amazed at how willing people are to subject themselves to all kinds of indignities in order to achieve their fifteen minutes of fame," he reflected.

Despite the differences among the three shows, he was pretty sanguine about the challenges, saying that the duties of a game-show host stayed pretty consistent regardless of the kind of program he was hosting.

"You still have to connect with your audience, and you

have to show respect for the material you're dealing with," he affirmed. "You have to act as a surrogate for the viewer and ask, 'What does that person in the living room want to know right now?'"

Of course, he still had his personal preferences. "I like there to be order on the show, but as the impartial host I accept disorder," he said.

Though he tried to remain above the fray, he sometimes found it difficult to hide his emotions, which was the precise moment a clear look of dismay would cross his face. "I have a way of looking at people that makes them feel uncomfortable," he admitted.

"That 'You've disappointed Daddy' is a tone I'm striking," he said, adding that it floats up most often when players miss a really easy clue: "How can you not get this? This is not rocket science."

Of course, some *Jeopardy!* episodes never quite get out of the starting gate, either because the contestants are palpably nervous or because their own easy categories are nowhere in sight. "Those games are tougher to host," he said, chalking it up to a bad day for everyone involved.

On February 3, 1991, Alex was finishing up the third of five episodes for *To Tell the Truth*—which was on the same five-show-a-day taping schedule that most game shows followed—when Jean called the studio to tell him that she had gone into labor. He dropped everything and ran to the hospital, and producer Mark Goodson filled in for Alex for the last two episodes.

Matthew Alexander weighed in at 8 pounds, 15 ounces,

and Alex was thrilled to be able to help with the delivery. He had become a first-time father at the age of fifty, with all of the joy—and fear—that entailed.

"One of the things that marriage and having a family has brought into my life is fear," he admitted. When he was single, he rarely worried about anything. Now, however, he had a whole slew of new worries to keep him up at night. And as a lifelong insomniac, he definitely didn't need the additional anxiety. He'd toss and turn before heading downstairs to read or do a crossword puzzle, and sometimes that would work. But when it didn't, he'd finally get to sleep toward dawn . . . just as the alarm clock went off. Not only did it make him cranky during the day, but he had a tendency to suddenly nod off, often while driving.

But with a new family, he felt that his fear was totally justified; after all, he had to be vigilant in order to protect them from every threat. On the flip side, a few months after he had become a father, he acknowledged that despite the fear, his newfound responsibilities benefited his work. "I've slowed my pacing way down," he said. "When I saw the first [episode of] *Jeopardy!* that I ever did, I was talking a hundred miles an hour."

His workload would slow even more. Soon after Matthew was born, Alex received word that both *To Tell the Truth* and *Classic Concentration* were being canceled. In his bachelor days, he might have been disappointed—and would have immediately looked for another job to fill the void—but now he clearly breathed a sigh of relief; it meant that he'd have more time to spend with his young family.

But fatherhood soon brought other fears to the surface: in

addition to the usual worries about whether he'd be a good dad and the challenges of dealing with an infant, he started to brood over what the twenty-four-year age difference between him and Jean might bring in the future. "When I'm an old man, some young stud might want my wife!" he complained.

Another worry had nothing to do with Jean: Alex was discovering that his memory wasn't as good as it used to be. Of course, he was at the age when little slips started to become noticeable and more common, but in his capacity as host of the brainiest show on the air, he was understandably concerned. "My powers of concentration seem to be diminishing," he admitted, and while he was able to chalk up some of his forgetfulness to working three game shows and becoming a new parent—coupled with his insomnia—his concern was mounting.

One day, he was flying cross-country when the in-flight meal was served. He looked down at his plate and was happy to see broccoli, which he loved, but for the life of him he couldn't think of the word "broccoli." He recalled, "I looked at it and looked at it, and that's when I realized that I was starting to lose it."

When he got back home, he contacted his doctor, who ran him through a battery of tests that thankfully revealed he was free and clear of any signs of either Alzheimer's or dementia. But he doubled down on his crosswords, whether or not he was suffering from insomnia.

Perhaps due to this scare, he decided to totally immerse himself in being the best father he could be. He looked to the many teachers who had appeared as *Jeopardy!* contestants for inspiration, and even described his job as being a teacher on the air. Teachers from all over the country regularly wrote to tell him that they'd adapted their lessons into an answer-and-question format, and that it made it much easier for their students to grasp the concepts.

"Teaching is a profession I greatly admire," he said, "and the thought of [Jean and me] nurturing and preparing a young human being for a successful adult life is very important to me."

He eagerly looked forward to showing Matthew what had mattered to him in his own life. "I always imagined that one of the joys of fatherhood was being able to teach your son the things you know," he said. But once he had welcomed a child into the world, his beliefs shifted. "His choices, and his life, will belong solely to him. I don't care what profession he chooses as long as he enjoys it."

With every passing day, Alex continued to be astounded by the personal changes that fatherhood had brought into his life. "For once, someone else's future matters more to me than my own," he said.

The same year that Matthew came into the world, Alex's family was about to expand once again, but not by having another son or daughter.

A few years earlier, Lucille had finally divulged her long-held secret to Alex and his sister, telling them that they had another sibling, a brother, whom she had had out of wedlock and given up for adoption when Alex and Barbara were both in their teens, thirty years earlier.

Alex was surprised, but also relieved to learn the truth, since he'd always sensed that his mother was coping with a secret burden. He hired an agency that specialized in locating adoptees, and though Lucille dreamed of being reunited with her son, she knew better than to get her hopes up; many children just didn't want to be found by their birth parents.

The agency searched for five years before locating her son, who was now named Michael and living in Belle River, Ontario, approximately 20 miles from Windsor, where Lucille had given birth to him.

Alex and Lucille were thrilled by the news, but also understood the trepidation and upheaval the news would create in Michael's life. They both thought it best that sister Barbara make the initial contact, to see if Michael would welcome his birth mother.

"I got a call from Barbara telling me about the whole thing," Michael said. "At the time, they talked about my brother Alex, but they didn't tell me who it was. They just said, 'We'll talk about it later.'"

Two weeks later, Lucille flew to Toronto, where Michael met her at the airport. He introduced Lucille to his family—including his adoptive mother—and later that year, Michael spent the Thanksgiving holidays in California with Alex, Lucille, and Barbara.

"When [we] sat around a table, you could really feel that we shared something, that there was something between us," said Michael.

Just as it was difficult for Alex and Barbara to grasp that they had a new sibling, Michael's children found it equally hard to fathom that they were related to Alex Trebek. "Sometimes I can't believe it myself," Michael admitted.

Best of all, Lucille had a huge weight off her shoulders; she had found her son, and she was happy and relieved to learn that he had thrived in the decades since she'd given him up for adoption. "Finding Michael has brought a peace to Mom's life that she didn't have before," said Alex.

Canada had always remained a huge part of Alex's life, even though he had not lived in the country for many years. Though his son, Matthew, automatically became an American citizen through birthright, Alex was reluctant to take that step himself. For one thing, even though he had long ago crossed "politician" off his list of future career possibilities, he still entertained the idea of entering politics in some form—perhaps an appointed office, not an elected one—at some point in the future, and if he became an American citizen, he'd have to give up the dream of ever doing so in his homeland.

But there was another reason for his hesitation. "I'm frustrated about American society," he admitted. "How can we be an affluent people and have homeless people on the streets?"

As a result, Alex doubled down on making appearances at charity events and donating money to organizations that helped the less fortunate. He expanded his sphere of benevolence to animals, specifically musk oxen, because he appreciated their instinctual nature when it came to protecting their families.

Musk oxen—essentially buffaloes with fur—are herd

animals. When a dangerous predator like a wolf appears in the vicinity, the adult males move the females and young oxen into a herd before arranging themselves in a circle that faces out so they can confront the threat head-on. "There are very few predators brave enough to attack this formation," said Alex. "Besides, I like the way their furry coats wave in the breeze when they are running."

In fact, after Matthew was born, Alex was so impressed by the animals' instinct to protect the herd at all costs that he and Jean decided to donate $10,000 each year to the Musk Ox Farm, a nonprofit group in Palmer, Alaska. He even signed on as the official ambassador for the organization, encouraging people to visit the ranch and learn more about the animals, and to "adopt" a musk ox in exchange for a donation. Then Alex sends them an official adoption announcement, which he personally signs as "Herd Godfather."

Once he had adjusted to the schedule of his newborn son, and with only one game show to host, Alex started to look for additional gigs again. With his Never Turn Down Work motto, some of the offers that came his way were a bit more unusual than others.

On March 24, 1991, he appeared at WrestleMania VII, not as a competitor but as a ring announcer and host, announcing the matches and interviewing wrestlers alongside TV talk-show host Regis Philbin. Marla Maples—then best known for the affair she had with Donald Trump while he was still married to his first wife, Ivana, and who would eventually become wife number two—came on board as timekeeper for the wrestling bouts, and Willie

Nelson serenaded the crowd with "America the Beautiful" to open the event.

As compared with his *Jeopardy!* persona, Alex appeared more energetic while chatting with the wrestlers, but he exhibited a palpable nervousness during his interview with Jake "The Snake" Roberts, who was known for bringing Damien, his boa constrictor, into the ring. When Jake held the snake out for him to admire, Alex quickly backed away.

He continued to pursue acting gigs on TV shows and in movies, but as was the case with his appearance on *Cheers* and *Mama's Family*, most of the offers that came his way were cameos where he played himself. He was good-natured about these roles—and accepted most of them—but he made sure the producers knew he'd be reviewing the script in advance to make sure that *Jeopardy!* was presented in a positive light and not ridiculed in any way.

He also cohosted the "Parade of Stars" telethon with singer Lou Rawls to raise money for the United Negro College Fund. And in a nod to his Canadian roots, he even laced up his skates to take part in a celebrity all-star ice hockey game, where his teammates included Matthew Perry and Jason Priestley.

Jeopardy! continued to thrive and expand; in 1993, Australia, Germany, the United Kingdom, and several other countries were airing their own versions of *Jeopardy!*, while the American show was rebroadcast in eleven countries.

For his part, while the format of the show didn't change, Alex believed it was important to shake things up every few years, from small tweaks like redesigning the game board to larger ones like introducing college championships and bringing the show to different cities in larger venues, where the dynamic would be different, because instead of the game being played out before a studio audience of around two hundred people, three thousand or more might be cheering on the contestants during the road shows.

Something else new was brewing: Jean was pregnant again, and daughter Emily Grace was born on August 17, 1993. Alex was thrilled yet again by his good fortune, but he still felt the pull of other activities where he'd learn something new.

First, he became involved in a winery. Though he had invested in Creston Vineyards in Creston, California, back in 1986, he became more active in the winery's operations in the Paso Robles region in the years that followed. With 250 acres spread over three separate lots, the vineyards grew enough grapes to make forty thousand cases of Cabernet Sauvignon, Chardonnay, Pinot Noir, and several other varietals. The vineyard had gotten its start in 1980, when Christina Crawford—daughter of actress Joan Crawford and author of *Mommie Dearest*—launched her own winery.

Though Alex prided himself on his wine knowledge, he wisely decided to leave the actual winemaking to the vintners and other experts. "I don't consider myself to be a wine connoisseur," he said. "I taste the wines, but not in the sense of holding veto power over the experts." He limited his opinion to either thumbs-up or thumbs-down, and nothing more. But he did admit that if he won a shopping spree in a supermarket, he would head first for the wine and spirits section.

After the winery came a horse farm, also in Creston. He bought the equestrian property—formerly known as Cardiff

Stud Farms—because he had passed the land on the way to the winery many times. "I fell in love with the property," he recalled, even though his chronic back pain meant that he couldn't ride a horse.

"I feel a little bit like Scarlett O'Hara's father," he said. "I have a deep-rooted feeling for land."

Alex had never thought he was interested in horses, at least not on a conscious level. But after he bought the 724-acre horse farm, he looked at the collection of horse-related items, including statues and works of art, that he'd amassed over the years, and realized that he'd always been a fan of everything equestrian.

He'd fully intended to use the farm to breed Thoroughbreds for clients, but a chance meeting with actor Jack Klugman, famous for playing the slovenly Oscar opposite Tony Randall's fastidious Felix in the 1970s TV sitcom *The Odd Couple*, sent him off in an entirely new direction.

Klugman had owned a racehorse named Jaklin Klugman that had come in third at the 1980 Kentucky Derby, and he told Alex that breeding was all well and good, but that he needed to take it a step further.

"He told me that what I was doing didn't compare to watching your own horse run in the Kentucky Derby," Alex said.

So over the course of the next few years, Alex went from having no racehorses to owning an even dozen, including a steed named Reba's Gold, who finished in the top two positions in half of his twenty-one career starts, earning over a quarter of a million dollars.

As was the case with the winery, after he signed the papers he left the logistics and operations to others. "I need the help of experts, because to me, all horses look beautiful," he said. He came to love visiting the farm for the peace he found on his visits. "Everything just slows down and is much calmer," he said. "It's like getting back to nature."

Another way he relaxed was by working on his new house. Whether supervising or jumping in with a hammer or power drill, he eagerly pitched in and liked to work alongside the carpenters, plumbers, and electricians so he could learn how to do something new.

Once the house was finished, he moved his family in—including mom Lucille, who moved into a carriage house on the property—and put his old house on Mulholland Drive on the market. "It'd make a great house for a bachelor or couple, or for families with kids over ten or twelve," he said, "but it's not a great house for toddlers."

The Mulholland Drive house sold in late December 1995, but with work on the new house complete, he needed a new project. He also wanted a tennis court, so he bought the house next door, because *Why not?* He used the tennis court and rented the house to retired baseball star Pete Rose from 1996 until 1999. For Rose, the best part of living there was having Alex as a landlord. "When something breaks, Alex comes over in work clothes and a *Jeopardy!* cap to fix it himself," he marveled.

In a way, Alex viewed his desire to design and build a new house for his family the same way that he regarded the male musk oxen that protected their herd. While of course he loved the physical labor of working on the house, he also viewed it as a way to honor his young family, especially his wife. "This house is all about Jean," he said. "I'm building it to build us a life, a house without history. In our other home, it was all about *my* taste in furnishings, *my* past. This house changes that."

Though he would always putter around the house, under-taking new projects just to satisfy his urge to keep busy—instead of cars, the three-car garage contained enough tools to fill the shelves of any hardware store—he was also very clear that, finally, he had found his home.

"This is my last hurrah," he said, "the last house I will ever build."

8

BEHIND THE SCENES

The fast-paced show you watch at home is a seamless production and never hits a snag. Some of the contestants might be in deer-in-the-headlights mode for a good part of the show, but the clues, buzzers, and questions go off without a hitch, and at the end, Alex has a congenial conversation with all three contestants as the fade-out music plays and the credits roll.

Of course, that's what the viewer sees. In reality, that sense of ease is a total illusion, never revealing the barely controlled tension of what goes on behind the scenes, which is even more incredible considering that five shows are taped back to back over the course of a few hours. There are stops, starts, last-minute changes and rearranging of clues just hours before tape time, wardrobe malfunctions, and instances where a contestant will insist he or she is right and the staff is wrong and the entire production will screech to a halt. Between the producers, camerapeople, writers, contestant coordinators, assistants, and all the other essential staff, about a hundred people work to bring every episode of *Jeopardy!* to the air.

Here's how it all happens.

The typical schedule is to tape five shows a day over two days a week—usually Tuesday and Wednesday—every other week to create forty-six weeks of original shows, including tournaments, before taking a six-week summer break.

Since Alex was never crazy about repeating shows that have already aired, for six weeks each year the repeated shows are usually tournament weeks. "If you know the correct response all the time, you're not as involved," he said.

Each season starts taping in late July for the first new shows, which will air in early September. All in all, the staff ends up working about nine months out of the year, though the writers and researchers work year-round.

Alex and announcer Johnny Gilbert—who before *Jeopardy!* came along, hosted an ABC-TV show from 1958 to 1960 called *Music Bingo* that was akin to *Name That Tune*—are the only employees who have remained since the 1984 relaunch.

From the beginning, Alex was always careful to describe *Jeopardy!* as a quiz show, not a game show, and himself as a host, not the star. Some might say he was just being modest, but he'd always believed that the role of a good game-show host was to steer viewers' attention toward the contestants, who he always regarded as the real stars of the show.

"If viewers think that I'm upstaging the contestants, they're going to resent that at some point, and I don't want to come off like a schmuck," he said.

At the same time, the responsibilities of a game-show host are more complex than they appear. "A game-show host is not just an announcer, he's the director onstage," said Alex. "The host has to have an eye for pacing, for keeping the game going. That's a role that not only takes maturity, it is one that the audience perceives requires maturity."

After more than thirty-five years with Alex at the helm, *Jeopardy!* is a well-oiled machine. But the only way he managed the grueling schedule was for the show to be taped at the same time every day.

Taping days start early for Alex. He gets out of bed at 5:15 and is in his Ram pickup fifteen minutes later for the half-hour drive to the studio in Culver City. Rather than listening to the news, he tunes the radio to SiriusXM for the hits of the '50s and '60s.

Around 6 A.M., he settles into his office, which is almost like stepping into a time machine to the 1980s: his office contains a television set that was new when Alex first came on board at the show, a VHS player and tapes, and a pencil sharpener. A sign on the wall reads, "I've got all the right answers as long as you have all the right questions."

He's quite proud of his Luddite tendencies. "I'm a pretty old computer, and slower because of it," he said. "I don't text, I don't access the internet, I don't blog, I don't tweet." He owns a cell phone, but it, too, is stuck in a time warp and he uses it just for calls. Though he does know how to use Jean's computer at home, he limits his use to mostly printing out boarding passes for flights.

He eases into his workday answering letters from fans,

and maybe doing the crossword puzzle in the newspaper. Around 7:30, he goes over the five games with all the answers and questions for that day's episodes. He'll check any clues for unusual pronunciations or if anything is unclear.

The clues are divided into four different subject areas: academic, lifestyle, pop culture, and wordplay, and the staff of eight writers and seven researchers find ideas and inspiration everywhere.

"Everything I read or see on TV or watch in a movie is fair game," said writer Michele Silverman Loud. "I feel like whenever I'm out doing something, I may stumble on a fact."

And one fact, event, or even a single word can often yield numerous clues. "I often tell people to look at a fact as a wheel with many spokes," said Alex, giving the Battle of Waterloo as one example. "Who lost? Napoleon. Who won? [The Duke of] Wellington. Then there's the year, the location . . . and suddenly you have four clues."

Many clues also contain occasional sly humor, which is often the part that virtually gives the answer away, according to executive producer Harry Friedman. "There's a little bit of a hint built inside most clues that will help you get to the correct response," he said. Plus, the humor turns what could start off as a boring clue into one to make both contestants and viewers—and Alex—smile.

Carlo Panno, a writer on the show in the 1980s and '90s, provides an example. "Obscure: MILLARD FILLMORE DIED IN THIS CITY. Better: MILLARD FILLMORE 'SHUFFLED OFF' THE PROVERBIAL MORTAL COIL IN THIS CITY."

The answer, of course, is Buffalo, New York.

According to Jules Minton, a former writer on the show, each clue also has to strike a particular balance. "Viewers should have one of two responses to a *Jeopardy!* question: 'I knew that,' or, 'Gee, I *should* have known that,'" he said.

It's important that the clues also entertain to a certain degree; there is such a thing as a boring clue. "Not all facts are interesting," said Minton. "The capital of Romania, for example—who cares what it is?"

The writers' jobs don't stop there, because each clue also has to physically fit into its individual screen on the game board; there are seven lines with up to seventeen letters per line, since certain letters—M, W, and O, for instance—take up more room.

Keeping all this front and center means that with the research, writing, and fact-checking, it takes a *Jeopardy!* writer about an hour to create each clue. On average, each writer creates one full category every day with six answers, with the expectation that one won't make the cut because sometimes Alex will take issue with a clue or category he thinks is just too difficult. "The biggest asset I bring to *Jeopardy!* is that I'm a common man," he said. "I have a pretty good sense of what people are going to know and are interested in, so I can say, 'This is too tough and nobody will get it.'"

Occasionally the writers will poke a little fun at Alex's determination to perfect his pronunciation of foreign words. Once they came up with a category they named "Aztecs speaking Welsh," and the clues were primarily made up of Aztec and Welsh words, which Alex called "a tongue twister's delight from the get-go." He approached one of the writers and said, "Damn, you guys gave me some really tough stuff today." The writer blew the cover when they burst out laughing and pointed to the date at the top of the card.

It was the first of April: April Fools' Day.

Even after all that, a great clue won't get on the air until it's double-checked. In other words, the researchers must verify that there's only one clear question for every answer. "We've got to back up sources twice," said Eric Johnson, a researcher on the show. "We essentially try to confirm that the first source was right."

And that could get expensive. In the 1980s and 1990s, when long-distance telephone companies charged for calls on a per-minute basis, phone bills at *Jeopardy!* were sky-high, because it wasn't unusual for researchers and writers to call sources all over the country—and the world, even—just to verify a single fact.

When Alex is finished with reviewing the games for the day, he meets with the writers and producers to voice his concerns over any clues or to ask them to clarify any where the meaning isn't crystal clear. They also check to see that there are no clues duplicated in any of the games; since the categories for each show are put together at random, it's not out of the question to have a clue about the same historical figure—like Benjamin Franklin or Queen Victoria—appear in more than one of the five games taped that day.

After the meeting, Alex returns to his dressing room around 10:30. "It's my job to transform him into the elegant host you see on TV every night," said Phil Wayne, who worked as Alex's stylist and wardrobe guru from 2008 until 2016. "To me, Alex looks best in a rich, dark suit," he said, adding that he favored dressing Alex in a particular Armani suit, but that a few Gucci suits hung in the dressing room as well.

"Alex likes shirts with stripes and patterns, and he loves a little check," said Wayne, who liked to coordinate his ties according to the calendar. "If it's Christmas, I'll make sure he's in red, and if it's Saint Patrick's Day, he needs to be in green."

Before Wayne took the job, Alex's stylist was Alan Mills, whose father was Don Mills of the Mills Brothers, a famous African-American family of singers with a long list of hits from the 1930s through the 1950s. Mills dressed Alex for the first two decades of the show, and he estimated that Alex wore over five hundred different suits over that time, marveling that in all those years, "His weight and measurements stayed exactly the same."

In recent years, Alex said, he pared his wardrobe down to just over a hundred suits.

Once Alex is dressed, coiffed, and makes a quick stop in the makeup chair, he heads to the studio around 11:15 for the first show of the day. Production of each show runs in real time—that is, the amount of time between the three rounds lasts exactly as long as the scheduled commercial breaks, so Alex is able to chat with members of the audience for only a few minutes.

And unlike hosts on other shows who appear as if they'd rather have a tooth pulled than banter with the studio audience, Alex admits that it's a favorite part of his taping day. "I really enjoy talking to the audiences," he said.

He believes that since they made the effort to show up,

he needs to engage them in the short amount of time they have together. "The people who come to a taping are entitled to something special, so you've got to give them something extra," he said. While some hosts retreat backstage or talk with a camera operator during the commercial breaks, Alex heads straight for the audience. "This is their only chance to see and hear me up close and personal, so I joke with them and they love it."

Most of the time, audience members will ask him about his mustache or what he thinks of Will Ferrell's impression of him on *Saturday Night Live*, but at one college tournament on the road, a woman stood up and asked, "Boxers or briefs?"

The audience twittered and then quieted down, waiting for Alex's response.

When he came back with "Thong," it brought the house down.

There's a fifteen-minute break between each taping, which allows Alex to duck back into wardrobe for his second suit of the day. He'll wear five different suits that day, since the shows will air on five consecutive nights. Players also bring extra outfits in case they win a game, but not more than three, since contestant coordinators believe that the audience won't remember—or care about—the outfit from their first game.

Just after noon, taping starts for the second show. *Jeopardy!* fans are often curious about what Alex is writing down at the podium, but it's nothing more than marking up the game card, putting a line through each clue after it's played so he knows not to read it again. Eagle-eyed viewers may notice that he uses a crayon; he previously worked with a Sharpie, but it squeaked too much so he switched.

Speaking of writing, one great mystery about the show is why contestants' handwritten questions on the screen during the Final Jeopardy! round look like, in the words of one critic, "a hummingbird having a seizure."

The answer: the pen is huge and unwieldy, and slippery when a contestant applies it to the screen. Longest-reigning *Jeopardy!* champion Ken Jennings compared it to "writing with an icicle on glass."

The third show of the day wraps up by two o'clock, at which point the studio audience leaves—they've been there for all three shows—and the staff and contestants have lunch. A new group of people will fill the audience for the fourth and fifth shows.

Taping for the Thursday show starts around three o'clock, with the last show forty-five minutes later. And just ten hours after he arrived at the studio, Alex gets in his truck and heads back to his family.

Even though he makes hosting the show look easy—especially after doing it for more than thirty-five years—every game is still a delicate balancing act during which Alex has to be on his toes every second that the cameras are running.

As the host, one of his primary responsibilities is to keep things moving along in what has become an increasingly fast-paced show over the years. He's explained that if he took even thirty seconds to provide a little anecdote about his day—or life—the contestants would get less time to play the game, which could mean the difference between winning and losing. At the same time, he's not an automaton, and needs to humanize both himself and the contestants, which is why he occasionally injects a very brief joke or takes a few extra seconds with a contestant to chat about an unusual hobby just before the Double Jeopardy! round. "I do want to keep it light, because it is a fairly serious show," he said.

And when it comes to those contestant chats, Alex has a simple formula: "Just pick something that throws them off a little, but that they're still able to talk about," he said. "Something like, 'I understand you're an ax murderer, but you got off. Tell me what happened.' Then a follow-up like 'Do you plan to throw axes again in competition?'"

But he doesn't hesitate to bring out his "You've disappointed Daddy" look when he feels it's called for. Even though it's old hat in these post–James Holzhauer days, Alex has never hidden the fact that he doesn't like it when players jump all over the board, which actually first became a thing way back in 1985 with player Chuck Forrest; the strategy is known as the "Forrest Bounce" for a reason. Essentially, some contestants refuse to start with the lowest-value clue and instead go right to the fifth clue in the category because they think they can earn a lot more money that way and also believe that it throws the other players off their game. Though Alex couldn't hide his annoyance, Forrest did quite well with the technique, winning five games and going on to compete in—and win—the Tournament of Champions in 1986.

Alex wasn't crazy about the method, not only because he thought that it messed with the way the game was originally designed, but also because it canceled out the natural progression that the writers often build into the clues. "The writers might've been trying to be really quirky and funny by naming the category a certain way," he said. "But if you start at the thousand-dollar clue or the two-thousand-dollar clue, you don't know what the category is about."

The tendency for players to latch onto the Forrest Bounce has ebbed and flowed over the years, but when it flares up, Alex has never hesitated to give his opinion. "It only works, *dickweed*, if you know the correct response to everything that's up there," he told Howard Stern in 2015.

Which is one of the reasons *Jeopardy!* has never aired live; besides the obvious need for a time-out in case a player calls foul on a clue, Alex has been known to let more than a few f-bombs fly over the course of the years. During a 2014 radio show, interviewer Dan Patrick told Alex on air that they were operating on a profanity delay. "I'm worried about your language," said Patrick.

There's also a highly viewed video montage of Alex cursing a blue streak while he was taping short promotional videos for *Phone Jeopardy!*, where fans of the show could play the game themselves—for five bucks *a minute*—by calling a 1-900 number back in 1990; it was clear that he'd rather have been doing something—*anything*—else. "After taping five shows on one day and five shows the next day, we were recording promos and I was not having a good time," he said. A YouTube user edited the video so certain phrases were repeated and it looked like Alex was drinking, which he disputed.

In any event, it's impossible to screen for players who will tend to jump around the board, and given that James Holzhauer employed the technique to spectacular results in early 2019—not to mention his tendency to bet his entire pot in the Final Jeopardy! round—the technique is definitely here to stay.

Even with the Forrest Bounce, a certain amount of well-rounded knowledge is necessary in order to succeed on the show. "It's more recall than anything else," said Maggie Speak, a producer on the show who's screened thousands of potential players at *Jeopardy!* auditions for more than two decades. "Good players are usually well-read and interested in a wide variety of things."

However, the show's contestant coordinators do screen potential players for other qualities. After they make it through the online test and are invited to an in-person interview and competition, the players who are energetic will definitely increase their chances of getting invited onto the show. "We interview you to find out if you have any personality," said Alex. "If you have no personality, then you can't be a contestant. You could be the *host* of the show, but not a contestant," he joked.

According to head writer Billy Wisse, contestants often get only one or two weeks' notice that they've made the cut and should get themselves to the studio for taping. One time, a contestant had essentially stopped eating and fainted during the show. It was one of the rare times when taping had to be stopped.

"Occasionally people will try and starve themselves to lose a few pounds," said Wisse. "It's tough up there. There are hot lights and they've never done this before, so we try not to say, 'How could you not know that?' or 'How could you make that absurd Daily Double wager?'"

•   •   •

Viewers and fans don't much like it when their beloved *Jeopardy!* is tinkered with, but as it turns out, most of the time both the staff and Alex feel the same way.

Even though computers had been a standard part of the American office landscape since the mid-1980s, it wasn't until 1998 that the writing and research staffs finally ditched the typewriters they had relied on since the show's relaunch in 1984.

Alex eschewed making any change unless he thought it would measurably improve the show. Though he occasionally studied other game-show hosts to see if they were doing anything that would improve his own hosting, he rarely saw something he could apply, except for segueing to a break. "Saying 'We'll be right back' can get tired," he said, "so I have borrowed new ways of doing that from the others."

Perhaps the biggest change to the show over the length of its run involves the category subjects. While Shakespeare and literature are still favorite go-tos for the writers, anything that involves classical music, Albert Einstein, or philosophy has become increasingly rare, whereas the buzzers go into overdrive when the answer is "Who is Taylor Swift?" or "What is twerking?"

"We probably have more American culture categories, and we think that has helped us appeal to a broader audience," said Alex.

For example, one notable category reflecting the new sensibility came in 2007 with "You Got Some Spleenin' to Do." "It was all about the spleen," said Alex. "We also had one category with clues about Homer, who wrote *The Iliad* and

The Odyssey, only the clues were read by Dan Castellaneta, who is the voice of the character Homer on *The Simpsons*."

"*Jeopardy!* is merely adjusting along with the evolving canon," Billy Wisse said in 2014. "Players don't know as much about Theodore Dreiser as they used to. It's sad, but there's not much anyone can do."

Even with the planning, researching, and fact-checking, it's inevitable that some things fall through the cracks. During a Final Jeopardy! round in April 1996, the clue was "At a May 1995 auction, a painting by her sold for $3.2 million, barely topping one by her husband."

All three contestants got it wrong with their answers: Mary Cassatt, Georgia O'Keeffe, and Grandma Moses. Alex then congratulated the winner and the closing credits rolled, but he neglected to give the correct question: "Who was Frida Kahlo?"

Irate viewers called their local stations as well as the *Jeopardy!* switchboard to complain. Did Alex forget to give the answer? Nope, the question was accidentally excised during the editing process.

Occasionally, Alex is the source of the goofs. "I've made some stupid mistakes," he admitted, though sometimes he'd tell tape editors to not fix it "so people will realize I'm human after all. I used to joke when we were first on the air that I didn't make any mistakes. Then for the next few years, I'd make a mistake but catch myself just as I was making it. Then I'd catch myself *after* I made the mistake. Now I don't even know when I make a mistake, I need other people to come up to me and tell me."

Even when he painstakingly researches those difficult-to-pronounce words and messes up anyway during taping, the mistake can be deleted during editing with the right pronunciation inserted.

Errors aside, the staff unanimously sings the praises of working at *Jeopardy!* And there's a reason why it's not unusual for employees to stay on the job for ten, even twenty years or more.

"Alex was one of the best bosses I ever had," said Carlo Panno, the former *Jeopardy!* writer, describing how Alex never hesitated to pitch in when necessary, even in the trenches. "Once, when we had a briefing on a new insurance plan, Alex answered the phones and booked contestants for an hour. He was the only one not on that insurance plan, being covered by AFTRA instead. He was thoughtful and intelligent, and I liked him a lot."

Alex's philosophy that everyone has something to teach him naturally extends to his coworkers on the *Jeopardy!* set. "It doesn't matter who comes up with a good idea," he said. "If it's a good idea, it's a good idea. You shouldn't let your ego get involved and say, 'I won't accept that idea from you because you're just a stagehand.' What kind of crap is that?"

And his natural curiosity to learn everything he can always came in handy when it was time to think up ideas for the annual staff holiday party. One year, Alex took the entire crew skydiving at a local indoor facility, and at another party the featured event was moonwalking lessons.

"There is no turnover here," said Alex. "Working for *Jeopardy!* is an annuity. You start and you go on forever."

9

BRANCHING OUT

By 1995, Alex had settled into his new family, and Jean had set about making a happy home for him.

Just as Alex's mother, Lucille, lived next door, Jean's grandmother had lived next to her family when she was growing up, and Jean was particularly close to her beloved grandmother, who was born in Norway. And just as Alex had adored having two Christmases every year when he was a child, Jean had also loved Christmas; she thought it was the most magical time of the year.

The preparations for it started shortly after Thanksgiving was over. Young Jean helped hang treasured family heirlooms on the branches of the Christmas tree, including carved wooden ornaments that her great-grandfather had made many decades before. She helped her grandmother bake cookies, carefully wrap gifts, and create paper snowflakes to tape to the windows. For Jean, the weeks of preparation served as a respite from her outsized responsibilities as the emotional caretaker for her family, and she absolutely delighted in the process every year.

Once she had her own family, Jean happily dove into rep-licating the same traditions while creating a few new ones as well. Early on Christmas morning, after opening their gifts, Alex, Jean, Matthew, and Emily would head next door, where Lucille would cook breakfast and the family would continue the celebration. After they finished eating, they'd open more presents before heading back to Jean and Alex's house, where they'd relax by watching some movies—including *National Velvet*, Jean's favorite—and dig into a *tourtière*, the same sa-vory French-Canadian meat pie that little Alex had looked forward to after midnight Mass on Christmas Eve.

Alex made it a point to keep his family as far away from Hollywood as he possibly could. And now that he had a fam-ily of his own, he no longer felt the pull to go out to grand openings and red-carpet premieres in order to be seen. He was much happier spending time with his wife and kids.

Once Matthew enrolled in school and started to play sports, Alex volunteered to help coach his soccer team. He taught the kids the rules of the game, and also told them they should play the game to win. When another parent voiced her concern about this attitude, Alex maintained that the kids played sports in order to absorb a variety of life lessons, from learning how to cooperate with teammates to wanting to excel. "Instill [the desire to win] in your child at an early age, but do it in a positive way, and not that he should do *anything* to win," he said.

Jean also decided to reach out into the community in a new way. In 1993 she started a flower shop with a friend in a former church in Santa Monica that they called The Flower Studio. They structured the business in an unusual fashion: it was open only by appointment, so customers had to book in advance to consult with the women about the most appropriate floral arrangement for a particular occasion. Jean and her friend, Janet, organized the business that way because they didn't want employees; plus, they were also both raising children, so they wanted hours that were fairly flexible.

While Janet handled the creative part of the business, Jean kept the books and also delivered the flowers, which she particularly liked because it allowed her to see how people reacted to the beautiful arrangements, which had a natural, almost avant-garde look to them.

The Flower Studio catered to many celebrities, and four years after it opened business was so good that the two women decided to open a regular retail storefront in Century City.

Alex was proud of Jean's business, and even though Alex eschewed Hollywood culture, he had long kicked around the idea of doing a version of *Jeopardy!* that featured famous people as contestants. The first incarnation of *Celebrity Jeopardy!* went on the air in the fall of 1992. Stars of the day like Carol Burnett, Luke Perry, and Regis Philbin took their turn at the game to win money for their favorite charities. The answers and questions were watered down somewhat, since the celebrity players didn't have to take the grueling entry test to qualify and most of the famous contestants were understandably nervous about the possibility of totally bombing on the air. "Showbiz is an ego business," said Alex. "No one wants to go out and look bad."

He admitted that the celebrity version of *Jeopardy!* was a lot looser—and more fun—than the regular shows. Plus, they took the shows on the road to places like Radio City

Music Hall, which could hold thousands of audience members. Since ratings tended to be higher than they were for the regular games, *Celebrity Jeopardy!* was a formula they'd return to again in the future. But Alex acknowledged that it provided a steep learning curve. "We have no idea how bright the celebrities are until they actually play the game, and at that point there's nothing we can do," he said.

In fact, many celebrities refused to go on the show, even though their appearance would have meant raising thousands of dollars for their favorite charity. "[They're] used to performing as other people, characters, and now all of a sudden they're on their own having to face tough questions," Alex explained.

Katie Couric has watched the show for years, but she won't go on *Celebrity Jeopardy!* "I'm [afraid I'll] choke and embarrass myself," she admitted.

During one *Celebrity Jeopardy!* tournament in 1995, Alex called out actress Lynn Redgrave because she had fallen way behind in the game. She told Alex that she thought her buzzer was defective. "It's not your signaling device," Alex snapped back, but immediately berated himself.

"My job is to run the game and help the contestants do their very best," he said, and he had clearly failed. "If I'm nasty, the audience will think 'Oh, he's being a smart-ass' and won't want me anymore." He vowed to be better aware of this in the future.

The celebrity who surprised him the most was comedian Cheech Marin of the comic stoner duo Cheech & Chong, who competed against anchor Anderson Cooper and actress Aisha Tyler in March 2010. Alex expected him to play true to type, but he was happily surprised to discover how wrong he was. "He was bright, very knowledgeable, and he won his game," he said.

Celebrity Jeopardy! plugged away for a while, but it became increasingly difficult to convince big stars to come onto the show. "More and more celebrities got frightened by the prospect of appearing on national television and embarrassing themselves," said Alex.

But an unexpected version of the show started to take off shortly after the first *Celebrity Jeopardy!* aired. Writers at *Saturday Night Live* clearly saw the comedic gold in putting the concept through their own lens, and in 1996 the live late-night show started running skits starring Will Ferrell as Alex, with members of the cast impersonating actors from John Travolta to Björk and with Sean Connery—played by Darrell Hammond—a recurring role.

Alex loved the parody. "It means you've arrived," he said. "It's a sign that you believe your audience will immediately recognize who you're poking fun at."

But his favorite take off on *Jeopardy!* came from comedy troupe Second City TV, where Canadian actor Eugene Levy impersonated Alex—his name changed to Alex Trebel—during a skit featuring a *Jeopardy!*-esque show called *Half Wits*. "He did the best Alex Trebek ever, better than Will Ferrell," he said. "He looked more the part too, with the dark hair and mustache."

With his reputation in American culture cemented with a parody on *Saturday Night Live*, Alex could have gone on automatic pilot, showing up to tape his ten shows every couple of weeks and just coasting the rest of the time like so many other game-show hosts did.

But that wasn't part of his DNA. As far as he was concerned, there was still a lot of life left to learn and experience. He rarely took advantage of his celebrity for his own gain, but he figured if he could bring others along on his journey of self-education, so much the better.

Classical music has been a category that players have found the most difficult on *Jeopardy!*, but Alex had always maintained an interest in learning more about it, as well as stepping into the shoes of performers, despite his lack of training. So he started to pursue opportunities where he could host fund-raising events for urban orchestras and opera companies. Sometimes he just showed up to give a speech, but it was a lot better when he was able to actively participate in a concert. Once he spread the word, he started to receive invitations to appear at concerts where he could provide narration for pieces like Saint-Saens's *Carnival of the Animals* and *Peter and the Wolf* by Prokofiev.

He also was a big fan of opera, and Rossini's *La Cenerentola*, based on the Cinderella story, was one of his favorites. Back in his bachelor days, he once learned that the opera was being performed in San Francisco the following evening, so he got on a plane and headed north just so he could see it. In fact, he loved *La Cenerentola* so much that he specifically searched for opportunities to host future performances of the opera, and was thrilled to participate in a presentation by the Austin Lyric Opera in 1989.

One night in May 1993, after contestants had completed a classical music category on the show, Alex mentioned that he'd always wondered what it would be like to conduct a symphony orchestra. The next day, orchestras from all over the country called to invite him to try it out. He sifted through the many offers, but in the end he chose a small orchestra in Greenville, Pennsylvania, because it was in financial trouble and Alex thought his appearance could help it out.

Once the date was announced, the event quickly sold out, raising over $40,000 in ticket sales. When Alex stepped onto the podium decked out in bow tie and white tails to conduct the sixty-seven musicians in a performance of his beloved *La Cenerentola*, as arranged for orchestra, he was beyond thrilled. "I think he did a very creditable job,'" said regular conductor Paul Chenevey. "And he seemed to be enjoying himself."

After handing the baton back to Chenevey, Alex took the microphone and stepped to the side of the stage to narrate Aaron Copland's *Lincoln Portrait*, in which the iconic American composer's music is accompanied by some of Abraham Lincoln's most stirring words.

Although Alex was no athlete—he prided himself on getting all the exercise he needed from working around the house—when he heard about the nationwide torch relay that preceded the 1996 Summer Olympics in Atlanta, he knew he wanted to experience it. Most of the 12,467 legs of the almost 17,000-mile route run throughout the United States were already assigned, but organizers found an open spot for him in Jacksonville, Florida, and off he went.

Though he was a little concerned about running the half-mile, he was buoyed by the crowds that lined the route to cheer him on, and he had a blast.

He continued to add to his guest-appearance résumé by

popping up on a variety of popular TV shows. As usual, he played himself, but it was clear he was getting weary of being typecast. "I'm comfortable being myself, but it got to be tiresome for me," he said.

"I wouldn't mind being [cast as] some evil person who tries to rule the world through superior brainpower," he added, joking, "People probably think I can do that anyway."

In 1996, he did get a chance to play against type on an episode of *The X-Files*, in the role of a villain known as a Man in Black, alongside former professional wrestler and Minnesota governor Jesse Ventura. After the show aired, one *Jeopardy!* contestant was so impressed that she asked Alex if she could touch his hand "because he had touched [*X-Files* star] David Duchovny."

Besides his desire to get cast as a villain, Alex also thought he'd make a good talk-show host, not to preside over a light gabfest like Merv Griffin did on his show, but doing something in a more serious vein. However, when he did get a chance to sit in for host Charles Gibson on *Good Morning America* for the week of August 15, 1994, he discovered that it was harder than it looked, and besides that, it took up a lot more time than his job on *Jeopardy!* did.

He was scheduled to talk to an author on the show, so he thought he should read the book in advance instead of relying on the press materials or having a production assistant read it and give him the CliffsNotes summary. So that took up several hours, and then he had to literally get up in the middle of the night to be on the set for a show that went on the air at 7 A.M. Perhaps the final straw was that he had to be enthusiastic on-camera about all the guests he'd meet and all the topics they'd cover. "I'm not all that interested in all of the things that they're going to throw at me," he admitted, so he was able to cross that ambition off his list.

With that settled, he became more open to being typecast, especially when it was in a slightly different form, such as on the animated series *The Simpsons* in an episode called "Miracle on Evergreen Terrace" that aired in December 1997. The story line was that Marge went on *Jeopardy!* to earn money but ended up at minus $5,200 at the end of the game and Alex told her she'd have to pay it back, whereupon she ran away from the studio.

On April Fools' Day 1997, Alex finally got the chance to see how the other half lived—the *Wheel of Fortune* half, that is—when he traded places with the show's host, Pat Sajak. There were only two contestants on *Wheel* that day—Sajak and hostess Vanna White—and all the solutions were *in*-jokes on the switcheroo: "Trading Places," "It's Not as Easy as It Looks," and "Pat, I'd Like to Solve the Puzzle."

Over on the *Jeopardy!* set, the categories in the first round were based on *Wheel of Fortune* categories—"Before & After," "Free Spin," and "Buy a Vowel," while the Double Jeopardy! categories were puns based around the word "fool."

A few years later, Alex was a contestant on a celebrity Halloween version of *Wheel of Fortune* in which he, along with skater Tara Lipinski and fitness guru Richard Simmons—who had replaced him at VTV—played the game while disguised to earn money for their favorite charities. Alex was dressed as a gnome, and it was difficult for viewers to figure out who exactly was wearing the costume. While he might have thought it was a breeze going in, he had a tougher time of it than he expected, primarily due to the fact that he was Canadian, where the letter Y is considered to be a vowel. When he asked Pat if he could buy a Y, everyone was momentarily confused before he got dinged for the faux pas.

In any case, Alex said that playing—and hosting—*Wheel* was a lot harder than it looked, and that he'd keep his day job for the time being.

Speaking of which, fans would occasionally ask Alex when he was planning to retire; after all, he was closing in on sixty, an age when many people are contemplating giving up their "day jobs." He said then, "Retirement is certainly something I'm considering, although I'm still having a lot of fun doing what I'm doing."

Besides, he realized that he looked a lot younger than he was. "I haven't had any plastic surgery, and every time I consider having it done, I think, 'Well, I'll retire from show business, so there's no need to do it,'" he said.

Even though he hadn't lived in Canada full-time for almost twenty-five years, Alex's opinions about his homeland still ran strong. He scoffed at the perennial Quebecois campaign for Quebec to become its own separate country. "It's naïve of Quebec to think that by forcing everybody to speak French, they're going to protect their language," he said. "Xenophobia never works. It hasn't worked throughout history and it isn't going to work here."

Despite his earlier misgivings about claiming American citizenship, in 1997 he decided to go for it—to become a dual citizen of Canada and the United States—primarily because his children were American by virtue of birth, but also because it would streamline his financial life when it came to paying taxes.

Other than that, his day-to-day life remained the same—though of course, shortly after the citizenship ceremony, he was called for jury duty.

With two passports to choose from, he had no excuse to stay home, and he and Jean introduced Matthew and Emily to the joys of travel from a very young age. And even though he was close to sixty years old, Alex still sounded like a little kid himself at the prospect of seeing a new place. "You're going to a different world—emotionally, spiritually, and physically," he marveled.

And when he traveled, he traveled light. "If you can't do a two-week vacation with one roll-on and a shoulder bag, you're not a good traveler at all," he said.

The same rules applied whether he was traveling with his family or not. "We're really low-maintenance—we never check our baggage, even if we're going on a safari in Africa for two weeks. The last time we were there, we took only two roll-on bags: one for the kids and one for us. People marvel at our packing skills."

As the year 2000 loomed, *Jeopardy!* was running as smoothly as ever, with millions of loyal fans tuning in every night. After more than a decade of hosting the show, Alex still enjoyed his primary job responsibilities as host. "The thing I enjoy the most is the thirty minutes when I'm onstage with our contestants running the game," he said. While he didn't mind his other tasks—checking over clues in the morning, meeting with staff—the highlight of his day was interacting with the players. "I just love being in the company of very bright people who are earning money the old-fashioned way, and they deserve it because they're bright, and that makes me feel really good."

But there was no mistaking the fact that most of those "very bright people" were not representative of the U.S. population as a whole, which was becoming increasingly diverse, and in late 1995, Alex ran into a skirmish with a beloved American poet and writer who was a fan of the show, but who said she had no choice but to boycott it.

"We have changed everything about this country, our very being here," said Maya Angelou on David Frost's PBS show in 1995. "And [when] I turn on a program like *Jeopardy!*, where quite often I am featured, or my name or some book I've written or some music I've written is the answer, I see no black people on it."

Though he did admit that contestants were usually white—and male—Alex said it wasn't for lack of trying. He explained that *Jeopardy!* regularly ran advertisements in African-American newspapers and exhibited at NAACP trade shows and meetings to encourage people to come take the test to qualify for the show.

"We suffer from a lack of talented black people trying out for the program," he said, adding that he thought the dilemma was similar to why celebrities didn't want to participate in *Celebrity Jeopardy!* "It could be that they're afraid of embarrassing themselves."

In the meantime, he stressed to the *Jeopardy!* writers and producers the importance of including clues and categories about African Americans on the show as often as possible.

"We are trying our darnedest to make America in general more aware of the accomplishments of black people in this country," he said.

In the early years of the show, producers also had trouble convincing women to become contestants on the show. Alex chalked it up to the traditional gender socialization of earlier generations. "Guys grow up very competitively," he said. "Men say, 'I can run faster than you, I can throw the ball farther than you,' while women are not used to competition, and instead say, 'Let's just talk. Let's get together and get along.'"

Plus, women who did well with the clues at home didn't see many women competing on *Jeopardy!*—at the time, there were three men for every one woman on the show—so it was almost a self-fulfilling prophecy.

This eventually changed, to the point where the scales became evenly balanced between men and women players, though Alex noted that women didn't gamble with their winnings as much as the men did. "Women consistently underperform with the wagering," he said. "They're more cautious, whereas men act like it's not real money until the end of the show."

Along the same lines, Alex was unhappy that no woman had ever hosted a successful game show, but pragmatic about the reasons, blaming it on a Catch-22 kind of situation. "If a woman was hosting a hit show for a few years, then you'd see more women hosting game shows," he said. "The problem is that women have hosted shows that haven't done that well—which includes a lot of guys, too—but [some people] use that as an excuse against women, blaming it on the woman instead of saying that the show wasn't very good."

In the meantime, *Jeopardy!* continued to diversify in other areas. Alex and some of the production staff thought the show might benefit by taking a road trip, increasing visibility and adding to its fan base, so in 1998, Alex took the show on the road, traveling to Boston, Washington, D.C., and even Stockholm, Sweden. Boston, in particular, was a huge hit. More than a hundred thousand people wrote in for tickets, but there was room for only twelve thousand, split among three seatings for the ten taped shows.

Alex had always been a vocal advocate for the U.S. military, and when the opportunity came up to hold *Jeopardy!* games at overseas bases, he thought it was a marvelous idea. The show teamed up with the USO, and Alex headed overseas to help administer tests to both officers and enlisted personnel, and everywhere the show traveled it was a big hit.

He liked to visit destinations that were often overlooked by the USO either because of distance or the small size of the base . . . or both. "You always hear about celebrities going over to entertain the troops when we're in a fighting situation, but where are they when we're not fighting?" he asked.

One year the show headed to Macedonia, where there was a tiny base with just thirty active-duty military personnel, so it was no surprise that the USO hadn't targeted it for a tour. Alex admitted that the logistics of booking a world-famous singer for a visit wouldn't work for such a venue, since the facilities couldn't support a large crew. But the nimble size of a *Jeopardy!* team—with a maximum of four staffers—worked to the show's advantage, and Alex was happy because he could spend time with men and women who were typically over-looked by USO performers.

He added to his workload in another rewarding way when he signed on to host the National Geographic Bee, an annual competition in which kids from fourth to eighth grade compete on a regional basis, with the winners traveling to Washington, D.C., to compete in a quiz-show format—not unlike *Reach for the Top*—to test their knowledge against other kids from around the country.

Alex loved it, because geography was one of his very favorite subjects in school. "Geography is about the future. History is about the past," he said. "Geography encompasses every aspect of your daily life without you realizing it. When you get in your car and you set up your GPS to find a restaurant or to take you to a location, that's a geographic event."

As an adult, he also understood the role a well-rounded knowledge of geography played when it came to all subjects. "If you know geography, then you know why civilizations developed where they did, why conflicts arose, and what the potential for different areas was," he said. "It covers everything, really."

On May 18, 1999, Alex celebrated his fifteenth anniversary as the host of *Jeopardy!* when he received his own star along the Hollywood Walk of Fame.

He continued to branch out that year, accepting numerous gigs to endorse a variety of products, from life insurance to milk and nutritional supplements. This was a bit ironic for a man who readily admitted he had Snickers and a Diet Coke for breakfast most days, though he did occasionally talk about his fondness for milk—low-fat in particular—especially as a way to deal with his insomnia. "I get up quite often in the middle of the night and I'll go to the refrigerator and I'll get a full glass of low-fat milk," he said. "I don't know why, but I've gotten into the habit. I've always liked low-fat milk."

So when the iconic "got milk?" campaign—featuring full-page ads with top celebrities wearing a milk mustache—approached him, he quickly agreed to be featured. The ads ran with the headline, "Your bones may be in jeopardy."

Alex also signed on as the company spokesperson for the vitamin and supplement company Rexall Sundown, appearing in magazine ads and TV commercials to demonstrate the company's new Twist 'N Learn line of vitamins, where he twisted an outer sleeve of the bottle to reveal the list of ingredients underneath.

His tenure at *Jeopardy!* was secure, and he had long been content to be in the number two position behind *Wheel of Fortune.* But in August 1999, a new show debuted that threatened to steal some of *Jeopardy!*'s thunder. Indeed, the prize money at *Who Wants to Be a Millionaire?* was more formidable—a million bucks for correctly answering the question in the final do-or-die round—but Alex wasn't worried, though he did publicly criticize both the game and the contestants for their lack of intellectual rigor.

"You have to wonder about some of the contestants on that show," said Alex, citing what he described as a typical question—"What's the usual color of Post-its?"—and the contestant's slack-jawed nonresponse. He also poked fun at host Regis Philbin, who had braved *Celebrity Jeopardy!* not once but twice and had finished last in both attempts.

Philbin came out swinging on his top-rated morning show *Live! with Regis and Kathie Lee,* inviting Alex to appear

on a future celebrity edition of *Millionaire*. "We'll put you in
the hot seat, and we'll see if you can remember what color
Post-its are!" he said.

Whether it was just good-natured ribbing between old
friends to goose ratings for both shows, or if it had been a
bona fide attack by Alex—whose show had outlasted dozens
of competitors that had launched and failed since he'd taken
the helm of *Jeopardy!*—was unclear. Either way, Alex put the
contretemps aside in order to focus on celebrating his upcoming tenth wedding anniversary with Jean, and marveling
at their successful relationship. "We're yin and yang," he said.
"We're opposites in many ways, but we think of the same
things at the same time. I'll think of something and she'll say
it out loud, or vice versa. I'll tell her to stop reading my mind,
but she'll say that she thought of it, too."

And they're both hard-core cocooners. "Basically, I'm a
homebody with my family, and I don't care if I never go out
in Hollywood," he said.

Life was indeed very good.

10

SHIFTING GEARS

Perhaps in response to the threat from *Millionaire*—perceived or otherwise—Alex decided it was time to shake things up a bit again at *Jeopardy!*, even though the show's fan base continued to grow, both in the United States and overseas. In 2000, there were local versions of *Jeopardy!* airing in more than thirty countries around the world.

Some more big changes took root in 2001. First off, the value of each answer was doubled; in the first *Jeopardy!* round, the value of each question jumped from a range of $100 to $500 to a range of $200 to $1,000, and more of those clues came in the form of short video and audio snippets. The color scheme of the set morphed into a more electric shade of blue, and tournaments aimed at specific demographics were added for teachers, college students, and even teenagers.

Producers also introduced the Clue Crew, a quartet of sidekicks who would travel around the world, recording video snippets for the show. More than five thousand people vied for the spots. "They brought us in to give the show a new look," said Sarah Whitcomb, one of the Crew's first members.

Another radical part of the show's gradual face-lift came in 2004, when one of the last bastions of Art Fleming's reign fell: if players won five games in a row, they were no longer booted off when the week ended, but instead kept playing until they lost. Eliminating the five-show limit was a good way to boost ratings, since viewers would be more likely to tune in each night to root for—or against—the reigning champ.

But perhaps the change that elicited the strongest response came in the spring of 2001, when Alex decided to shave off his mustache on the spur of the moment.

It was a tape day, and four shows were already in the can. Alex was in the makeup room for a touch-up when he looked in the mirror and told the makeup artist that he was going to shave his mustache.

When?

Now. He picked up a razor and shaved off half of it. "How would it be if I walked out now?"

"Not a good idea."

So he shaved off the other half and headed back out to the studio to tape the last show of the day. He later admitted that he wasn't sure how many people noticed the difference.

When he got home, he greeted Matt and Emily, then ten and seven, in their playroom (which they referred to as the Play-Doh Room). "I stood in the doorway and I said, 'Hi, guys,' and they said, 'Hi, Dad,' and Jean asked how taping went that day."

They chatted for ten or fifteen minutes, and nobody said

anything about his newly shorn face. Alex finally asked, "Do you notice anything different about Dad today?"

They looked up. Jean said, "Oh my God, you shaved your mustache," and Matthew immediately began to wail.

Thankfully, everyone eventually adjusted, but when *Jeopardy!* fans finally noticed, Alex was clearly caught off guard by the reaction to the disappearance of his facial hair, and he was more than a little annoyed. "Look at what's going on in the Middle East, and at this natural disaster, and they're asking about my mustache," he complained.

There were other changes in the works as well. He decided to start paring down certain parts of his life, selling his stake in Creston Vineyards in 2001. Though he was drinking less, Alex hadn't lost his fondness for wine; he just wanted to have more time for other pursuits, particularly increasing his travel around the world, both for himself and for the charities and nonprofits he supported. Besides, he'd ended up taking a bath on his investment in the winery, losing more than two million dollars by the time he severed ties. "I think it was the only winery in California that didn't make money," he said. "But I got to enjoy the wine, at least."

There was one change that hadn't escaped the notice of long-time fans. "Viewers have told me that over the past twenty years I have mellowed as a host," he said, wholly attributing it to Jean's influence. "She's softened me. I try to be more understanding when players make mistakes, to ease the blow for them."

It was a hard habit to break. "People still have a view of me as being kind of aloof, maybe a little smart-alecky," he said.

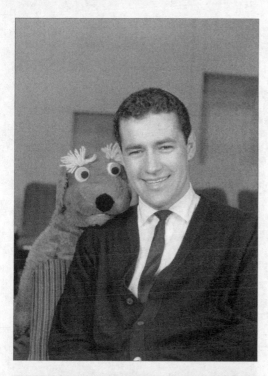

Alex (right) and Mike the Mutt, from *Vacation Time*, a CBC children's show, hang out in 1964.

(Credit: *CBC Still Photo Collection/Roy Martin*)

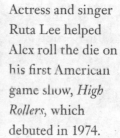

Actress and singer Ruta Lee helped Alex roll the die on his first American game show, *High Rollers*, which debuted in 1974.

(Credit: *NBC publicity materials*)

In 1975, Alex was a presenter at the *2nd Daytime Emmy Awards* with *General Hospital* actress Rachel Ames.

(Credit: *Ann Limongello /Walt Disney Television via Getty Images*)

Alex and his first wife, Elaine Callei, attending a black-tie event in 1976.

(Credit: *Frank Edwards/Fotos International/Getty Images*)

Alex in the early years of *Jeopardy!*, still looking like he can't believe his good luck.

(Credit: *Globe Photos Inc./ImageCollect.com*)

Pat Sajak, Vanna White, and Alex all worked for Merv Griffin, the actor/singer/talk show host who dreamed up the idea for both *Wheel of Fortune* and *Jeopardy!*

(Credit: *Globe Photos Inc./ImageCollect.com*)

Alex and Jean enjoy a moment with their young son, Matt.

(Credit: *Photo supplied*)

Alex costars with Jesse Ventura as Men in Black in a 1996 episode of *The X-Files*.

(Credit: *FOX Image Collection via Getty Images*)

Alex receiving his star on the Hollywood Walk of Fame in 1999.

(Credit: *ImageCollect*)

Alex with Jean and eight-year-old Matt and five-year-old Emily after receiving his star on the Hollywood Walk of Fame in 1999.

(Credit: *Rose Prouser/ Reuters*)

Always seeking to help others, Alex was one of many celebrities who appeared in the iconic *got milk?* ad campaign, which doubled as a kind of public service announcement and commercial for the dairy industry in the late 1990s.

(Credit: *Ad supplied*)

Alex traveled with the USO to Kadena Air Base, Japan, in September 2007, to visit with troops and film clues for future episodes of *Jeopardy!*

(Credit: *U.S. Air Force photo/Senior Airman Nestor Cruz*)

Alex raced at the 33rd Annual Toyota Pro/Celebrity Race in Long Beach, California, on April 7, 2009.

(Credit: *Carrie-Nelson, ImageCollect .com*)

Matt, Nicky, Emily, Jean, and Alex appear at the *38th Daytime Emmy Awards* in Las Vegas in 2010.

(Credit: *WENN Rights Ltd/Alamy Stock Photo*)

Alex communes with an equine friend in 1997.

(Credit: *Donaldson Collection/Michael Ochs Archives/Getty Images*)

Alex and Jean attend The Night of 100 Stars Oscar Viewing Party in Beverly Hills, California, in February 2015.

(Credit: *Carrie Nelson/Shutterstock. com*)

"But if somebody gives you an incorrect response, how do you correct them without appearing authoritative and, in the minds of some people, a little snobby?"

He also found it difficult to keep from cheering on a contestant coming from behind. "But I'm like the parent with three kids—I can't show favoritism," he lamented.

Another change came when Alex and Jean bought a home on Lake Nacimiento near Paso Robles to use as a vacation getway. The family reveled in the seclusion of the lake house, which allowed them to continue their homebody ways just over two hundred miles north of their home in Los Angeles.

They spent weekends and school breaks at the lake house, swimming, boating, and hanging out inside with videos and board games on rainy days. "We were nurtured by Mother Nature herself—no internet, no cable, no malls, no movie theaters, no restaurants," said Jean. "[Instead] we were entertained by the most glorious oak trees, deer, and birds of all sorts."

Of course, Alex found it difficult to just do nothing, so while he went Jet-Skiing on the lake and rode an ATV with the kids on trails nearby, back in Los Angeles, whenever he wasn't working or traveling for World Vision or the USO, he was working on the house, both inside and out. In fact, he had become so accomplished at tackling complex repair jobs that while previously he had learned the art of home repair from watching the plumbers and electricians who came to the house, it wasn't unusual for them to watch how he performed a particular task, or for him to provide advice on a new technique to the experts.

It didn't hurt that he had a well-equipped workshop, and

regularly visited hardware stores to stock up on tools and equipment that he might just need someday. Once he even bought out the stock from a store that was closing, even if he wasn't clear on the purpose of a particular flange or clamp. And he joked that he had an official Home Depot Shopper of the Month certificate hanging in his den.

One time a plumber came to the house for a job and was short on the materials needed to fix a leak. So Alex headed out to his three-car garage, stocked with tools and bins filled with nuts, bolts, nails, and every kind of hardware imaginable, and handed the plumber some one-and-a-quarter-inch copper pipe and a ball valve, enabling the plumber to finish the job.

Alex took particular pride when it came to the automatic watering system for the lawn. In fact, he adopted the nickname "Mr. Sprinkler Man" because of his skill at fixing it. "I take a great deal of delight in repairing all that stuff, and in being wise to the sensitivities of my home," he said.

"I always thought that the best way to get something done was to do it yourself, because you could do it faster."

He even joked that he should start a business on the side, and he already had the perfect name for it: "Is your house in Jeopardy? Have tools, will travel."

But occasionally there were harsh repercussions to doing the work himself: It's been the cause of many of his injuries through the years, from dropping a jackhammer on his left foot to falling off ladders, which he acknowledged was his biggest nemesis. "They will abandon me at the weirdest moments," he acknowledged.

"I'm constantly injuring myself, and sometimes I don't

notice until an hour later when I'll say, 'Geez, I'm bleeding. How did that happen?'" He admitted that he didn't help matters when he neglected to wear a baseball cap while fixing something in the attic. "You never see that beam above you!" he explained.

Despite the dangers, he planned to continue working on the house, maintaining it was the only way he got any exercise. "I don't believe in exercise for the sake of exercise," he said. "If I'm going somewhere, I will walk, but if I don't have to go anywhere, I'm not likely to get on the treadmill."

Though his practice of having a diet soda and a candy bar for breakfast didn't make Jean happy, he'd occasionally choose a granola bar instead, or a donut, which he viewed as a healthy alternative.

"I do have a good solid dinner every evening, but I find that there must be some kind of camel blood in me, because if I'm doing physical labor I never think of food [or water]," he said, while admitting that this often backfired later in the day when his muscles spasmed and strained.

His insomnia continued to be a problem, and in January 2004 he was up at the lake house driving his 1991 white Ranger pickup when he fell asleep at the wheel. He plowed through a row of mailboxes and flew about forty feet over a ditch before hitting a utility pole and coming to a stop.

When California Highway Patrol Officer Scott Koolman arrived on the scene, he didn't recognize Alex until he saw his driver's license. He asked him if he'd been drinking, and Alex said he hadn't, that he just hadn't slept the night before. The truck was totaled, but amazingly, he wasn't injured and walked away from the crash.

A few months later, there'd be another incident to shake up Alex's world, which arrived in the form of a thirty-year-old software engineer from Salt Lake City.

Ken Jennings began his record-smashing seventy-four-game winning streak innocuously enough.

The first day he won $37,201, an impressive figure. By his fifth day of play that figure had grown to $156,000. Then, thanks to the lifting of the five-day rule, he returned for a sixth day.

On day seven, he surpassed the record-setting amount Tom Walsh had won—almost $187,000—over his eight games in January 2004.

Sometime during Jennings's thirtieth game, on July 13, 2004, he reached the million-dollar level. Brad Rutter had cleared just over $1.15 million playing in the 2001 Tournament of Champions, and set a new record when he won the Million Dollar Masters Tournament in 2002, but the dollar amount of the prizes was higher during those events.

Fans—and critics—immediately took notice. One reviewer compared Jennings to a robot as he zeroed in on his "lightning-fast finger and computer-file memory." Several experts figured out that Jennings came up with the right question a whopping 85 percent of the time; his winning streak also had the side effect of making his competitors even more nervous than they already were.

The show clearly benefited from Jennings's continued appearances, with ratings jumping 25 percent in just the first month. Websites about TV game shows also reported increased hits since Jennings had taken over the airwaves.

Alex, for his part, was alternately enchanted and annoyed with Jennings.

"Ken was the perfect contestant," he said. "He was bright, he understood the game, knew how to play, he understood the nuances, knew how to wager, and was funny."

Though Alex has maintained for years that the contestants are the real stars of the show and he's merely there to serve as facilitator, when it was clear a contestant was stealing his thunder, he became a little testy. "It became the Ken and Alex Show," he admitted.

And he had one other qualm about Jennings's winning streak. "I was spending more time with Ken Jennings than I was with my wife."

Jennings's success affected the show in some weird ways. For one thing, during the informal chitchat sessions at the beginning of every show, after the first month or so Alex and Jennings resorted to digging for offbeat topics in order not to repeat themselves. "I couldn't think of any questions to ask him anymore," said Alex. Indeed, somewhere around week six, Jennings filled the getting-to-know-you segment by admitting that he was fond of meals served on airplanes.

But there was a delicious tension as well. At the beginning of each show, Alex—and the rest of America—always wondered if *this* was going to be the show when the mighty Jennings fell. But as he continued to win on into summer and the end of the season—with a hiatus of a couple of months before new shows appeared in the fall—Jennings's acumen and skill with the buzzer, often the trickiest part of the game to master, showed no sign of slowing down. If he had an Achilles' heel, it was in categories around hockey and country music, which accounted for the majority of his muffed questions. "Anything with a mullet . . . and I was done," he said.

There was no stopping him, and long-established records continued to fall. September 15 marked his forty-third show, breaking the previous record set by a game-show contestant. He won his fiftieth show on October 5, and on November 3, he became the top-earning game-show winner in history, with $2.197 million in cash.

But as it turned out, the end was in sight, and the moment his fans, detractors, and future competitors had been eagerly awaiting—or dreading—finally came. On the episode that aired on November 30, 2004, after winning seventy-three games in a row, Jennings started the game feeling a bit out of sorts.

"I couldn't find my groove," he said, attributing his nerves to the fact that his parents and in-laws were in the studio audience. And earlier that day, he had possibly jinxed things by saying out loud that his winning streak couldn't last forever.

The first two rounds went smoothly enough, but then the unthinkable happened: not only did he flub the Final Jeopardy! question—to the clue "Most of this firm's seventy thousand seasonal white-collar employees work only four months a year," Jennings responded, "What is FedEx?"—but his bet placed him in second place when Nancy Zerg, a California real estate agent, aced the question with "What is H&R Block?"

He still had earned more than $2.5 million over the course of the show, but when he contacted his wife, Mindy, to break the news, she instantly realized what had happened. "When

Ken called in the middle of the day, I knew it was over," she said. "They never let you call while they're taping, not unless you lose. My first thought was 'But Ken doesn't lose.'"

When the dust had settled, Alex marveled at Jennings's feat. "I very much doubt that we will ever see an accomplishment like this again," he said.

But Alex was also surprised at how emotional he became when it was clear that Ken wouldn't be returning to the stage. "I had a tear in my eye, I really did," Alex admitted. "Ken's gone. My buddy, my pal."

Jennings later said that it took a while for reality to sink in, and that he felt a bit disoriented at first. But less than twenty-four hours after his losing show aired, Jennings was on the talk-show circuit. The agreement that every *Jeopardy!* contestant signed dictated that they couldn't tell anyone they'd lost—including the media—until after the losing episode aired. Once the news broke, Jennings spoke with a flurry of newspaper reporters and booked appearances on national TV shows, including *Late Night with David Letterman*. He also signed a book contract and started to sift through the endorsement deals that came flooding in.

H&R Block came calling, too, offering to provide Jennings and his family with free financial advice for the rest of his life; a spokesperson estimated that Jennings would owe a minimum of one million dollars on his *Jeopardy!* earnings.

But the first thing he did when the check arrived was surprisingly understated. "We had a very old, very crappy TV, and I went out and bought a big wide-screen TV so I could see every pore of Alex Trebek," he said.

Ratings for the show had increased 22 percent over the

previous year, even beating *Wheel of Fortune*'s viewership for a few weeks. *Jeopardy!*'s staff members were pleasantly amazed that there was so much buzz over a game show that was two decades old.

The producers—and Alex—wanted to ride that train a bit longer, and so a month after Jennings exited the show, it was announced that a Super Tournament would be held the following year, where more than a hundred winners from the previous twenty years would compete in a showdown. The code name for the tournament was "The Quest for Ken."

"Ever since Ken started his amazing run, people have been speculating on how some of the past *Jeopardy!* players would do against him," Alex said, adding that the tournament would be one way to find out.

The stakes would be much higher: The winner would win two million dollars, and the runner-up would receive a cool half-million. Third prize was $250,000.

The Ultimate Tournament of Champions ran for seventy-six shows—two episodes longer than Jennings's winning streak—from February through May 2005, and this time around the winner was Brad Rutter, a champion from 2000 who had played when the five-game limit was in effect; Jennings came in second. But both Rutter and Jennings would frequently return to future tournaments, where they would trade places as the top money winner several times over the next decade.

As 2005 dawned, Alex continued his two-week routine of two days of taping and then twelve days to do with as he pleased.

Even as he celebrated his sixty-fifth birthday, he showed no signs of announcing his retirement.

Of course, given his work schedule, he had the absolute luxury of spending twelve days recovering, but he couldn't sit still. He spent time puttering around his house, pruning trees, and driving to Home Depot; his taping schedule, he reflected, served as an anchor around which he could schedule the rest of his wide-ranging activities and interests. "[Jean] mentioned recently that when I'm not taping, I tend to fump around a little, like, 'What am I going to do today?'" he admitted.

The side gigs he picked continued to reflect his eclectic interests. He appeared on the animated series *Family Guy* and had a small role in the 2007 movie *The Bucket List*, which starred Morgan Freeman and Jack Nicholson as a couple of terminally ill friends who figured they have nothing to lose and decided to check off all the things they'd wanted to do their whole lives. Freeman's character was a die-hard *Jeopardy!* fan who dreamed of competing on the show.

"I read that script, and I had tears in my eyes," said Alex. The original script had Freeman appearing on the show and dying in the middle of a game, but the producers deleted the scene and Alex's cameo never came to pass.

Matthew and Emily were starting to blossom into their teenage years, developing their own personalities and interests, and Alex and Jean were always right there to help in any way they could.

While Alex was never known to be an adventurous eater— "[Dad] would be fine eating chicken, white rice, and broccoli for the rest of his life," Matt quipped—his son clearly liked to explore a wide variety of cuisines. While still a teenager, he headed off to farmers' markets to sample different dishes, grilling the cooks about the ingredients and techniques they used.

Emily, on the other hand, was heading down a favorite path of both parents: working on houses. Emily had seen Dad doing repairs in and around the house, and Jean had been working in commercial real estate when she and Alex met, so not surprisingly, their daughter had been fascinated by houses from an early age, and as a child she dreamed of being an architect.

She had learned to fix up things around the house by spending time with her dad, just as Alex had absorbed reams of home-repair expertise by watching and working alongside his uncles. When she was around sixteen, Alex was teaching her how to drive a car, and one day she was practicing in the yard and ran over one of the in-ground sprinklers. "We all knew Dad would be out five seconds later fixing it," she recalled.

The following year—2006—was a year of milestones for both Alex and his long-running show.

In June he was inducted into Canada's Walk of Fame in Toronto, alongside the actors Eugene Levy and Brendan Fraser and musician Paul Shaffer. "It's truly an honor to be recognized by your own country," he said.

That same year, *Jeopardy!* introduced online testing to recruit a more diverse pool of contestants, as Alex had clearly taken Maya Angelou's criticisms to heart. Previously, the show would send a crew of staffers to a particular city and potential candidates could either send in a postcard for a shot at taking the test in person or show up at the auditions to grovel before the audition team.

Online testing changed all that. "The show is better for it. America was full of people [who were] super-good at *Jeopardy!*, but they weren't going to drive to the mall to fill out a contestant audition card," he explained.

Then, just before Christmas 2007, Alex landed in the hospital—not because he dropped a sledgehammer on his foot, but for something more serious.

At first, he thought he had strained his back working on the house earlier in the day. But the pain increased, and Jean insisted on taking him to the hospital, where doctors told him he'd had a heart attack. He spent a few days in the hospital, and thanked his fans for all the cards, letters, flowers, and phone calls that had arrived during his stay, which had caught him by surprise.

"There's a bit of a cynic in me, I'm a skeptical person, so I'm always surprised by the kindnesses of strangers," he said. The incident caused him to reflect on his own actions in the past. "There are many times in my life when I have missed an opportunity to do a kindness, and I have regretted it afterwards."

Another tragedy hit that same year when his sister, Barbara, died of cancer at the age of sixty-five; Alex and Lucille were with her when she died. She'd dealt with several forms of cancer over her lifetime—including breast cancer—and she didn't hesitate to place the blame on their childhood home of Sudbury.

"Barbara said because Sudbury was a nickel-mining town,

there was a high rate of cancer among people in the area, including their relatives," said former husband, Barton Holcomb.

Perhaps prompted by Barbara's death, both Jean and Alex started to stretch themselves just a bit more than before.

Though Jean was always quite spiritual, she started to explore different religions specifically to learn how she could use their tenets to help other people. She was particularly attracted to a denomination known as Religious Science, which incorporates traditions from a variety of religions while mixing in positive thinking, gratitude, and meditation. In fact, Jean felt the tenets benefited her so much that she became a licensed practitioner at the North Hollywood Church of Religious Science, where she counseled others.

She combined her religious practice with gentle forms of healing, including Reiki and sound healing, where she used her own voice in tandem with a series of graduated bowls to create sounds that can help calm people. "The human voice has so much power and healing, like when a mother sings a lullaby to her baby," she said.

Alex's love of travel continued to play a vital role in his life, albeit in a slightly altered fashion. While previously he was content to do solo trips to benefit World Vision or the USO, he decided it was time to invite loyal fans to join him on these excursions. In June 2005, he was the star attraction on a cruise with the Seabourn Cruise Line, featuring an itinerary that included the Baltics, Russia, Scandinavia, and Germany. And in 2009, the show held a sweepstakes to select several lucky winners to sail to the Galapagos Islands on a cruise with Lindblad Expeditions and mingle with Alex, who would shoot video and clues for upcoming shows.

Perhaps as a reaction to his heart attack, Alex decided it was time to check a few things off his own bucket list, which included everything from skydiving to flying in an F-16 fighter jet. "I'm willing to try everything once," he said.

In 2009, he signed up for the Grand Prix Celebrity auto-racing circuit in Long Beach, California, where he had a definite strategy for winning without passing and while keeping to a decidedly poky 80 miles per hour in a car designed to easily travel at speeds three times as fast.

"I'm just going to wait for everyone to crash, and then go by them," he said. "It's very dangerous to pass people. Then again, I don't pass too many people on the freeway either."

11

GIVING BACK

In addition to checking things off his personal bucket list, Alex wanted to do more when it came to helping other people. "[Jean and I] have all the money we need to live and we can't take it with us, so if there are groups in need, we try to help them," he said.

While his charitable streak and desire to give back had always been strong, Jean encouraged him to think about giving in a new way. "She has taught me the value of looking outside of yourself in a charitable way, helping others either financially or personally, and never expecting anything in return," he said.

He loved to share his money and time with organizations, but it could become a bit unwieldy. "When you send in donations, pretty soon you are deluged," he said. "You write one check and soon you'll hear from every other charity on God's green earth. They're all worthwhile, of course, but you have to make a few decisions."

In 2011 Alex and Jean launched the Trebek Family Foundation as a way to both streamline and ramp up their giving; the foundation made it possible to fund projects on a much larger scale than before.

Some of the funds were steered toward the educational facilities that had helped both him and his children, who were now grown and forging new lives. Matt graduated from New York's Fordham University in 2013 with—emulating his dad—a degree in philosophy, and Emily graduated from Loyola Marymount in Los Angeles in 2015 with a degree in design and architecture. Alex and Jean were fiercely proud of both their children.

"They're really sharp, and have done their due diligence in their respective endeavors," he said.

"They're both very compassionate, sensitive people," Jean said. "They're really the best of Alex and me."

Through their foundation, Alex and Jean donated a million dollars toward scholarships and financial aid at Fordham for undergraduates who live in North Harlem, New York, traditionally a neighborhood that has a high percentage of people living in poverty.

"I have seen the benefits of a Fordham education close up," Alex said, citing Matthew's positive experience and growth at the university. "My hope for this scholarship is that it helps many other deserving students have that same transformational experience."

The foundation also gave five million dollars to his alma mater, the University of Ottawa, to launch the *Alex Trebek Forum for Dialogue*, which encourages public policy debate and research across Canada. And after spending a quarter-century presiding over the National Geographic Bee, he marked his last year of hosting with a donation that doubled the first prize from $25,000 to $50,000.

He discovered that he loved giving away large sums of money to organizations, knowing that it made a significant difference in the lives of many people. "It gives me a great deal of joy."

To mark three full decades of volunteering with World Vision, Alex adopted a small village in Zambia and pitched in for several weeks, helping to construct schools and a health clinic, and fixing up homes. He was appalled at the lack of sanitation and clean drinking water. "The village of about seventeen hundred used the same dirty water hole where cattle were drinking," he said. His donation resulted in eight new wells being drilled for the village.

"If I'm going to do something, I'd like it to make an impact, and I'd like to know who it is making an impact on," he said. "So the smaller the area of help, the better it is."

Back at home, the name of the game at *Jeopardy!* was still small changes here and there, but in 2011, when the idea of having a nonhuman contestant stand at a player's podium came up, Alex had his doubts.

Inviting an IBM computer named Watson—after Thomas J. Watson, the company's founder—was definitely a novel idea. Ever since a supercomputer code-named Deep Blue had defeated world champion chess player Garry Kasparov back in 1997, the computer firm had been looking for another computer-human matchup to show off the strengths of its technology. *Jeopardy!* was a natural fit.

It wasn't the first time the show had been approached

about such a competition, but other developers and technology companies hadn't been able to figure out how to program either natural language or the quirks of human communication, including normal sentence structure as well as nuance, subtext, and jokes, all of which are on prominent display every night on *Jeopardy!* So while programmers could feed encyclopedias, newspapers and magazines, every song lyric ever written, and billions of other facts and events into a database, the computerized contestant had to also be able to interpret the clues the way a human would, which meant the occasional dose of snarky humor, as well as being able to translate a foreign word into English whenever the writers decided to subject Alex to a few pronunciation tongue twisters.

Plus, the supercomputer had to master the buzzer, as well as know how to place large wagers to have the best chance of beating Rutter and Jennings.

Watson—which consisted of more than four hundred servers at an IBM base in New York State—could do all that and more, or so the mad scientists behind him/her/they claimed.

At the very least, it would make for great TV, and Alex and the producers upped the ante by bringing back Ken Jennings and Brad Rutter to compete against Watson over three nights during the February sweeps.

Jennings was realistic about his chances. "If you beat the gajillion-whatever supercomputer, you're a hero," he said. "But if you lose, it *is* a computer, so I guess you did the best [you could] for your species."

Watson was the winner in all three shows, winning $77,147, while Ken accumulated a puny $24,000, and Brad amassed just $21,600. Alex later disclosed that Watson was easily his least-favorite contestant of all time. "Though I've never encountered a contestant that I took a dislike to, some I didn't like as much as others," he admitted. "As far as taking a dislike to a particular contestant, [it was] only Watson."

But he was serious about the influence that Watson would have on the future. "I'll be impressed when IBM develops a robot that can host *Jeopardy!*," he said. "I guess that's not too far off."

Alex continued his schedule of traveling for both charity and personal pleasure, but he often took gigs where he'd give talks and emcee games for large corporations around the world. Jean would frequently accompany him on these short business trips.

In July 2011, they were staying at the San Francisco Marriott Marquis so he could host a geography competition called the National Geographic World Championship, to be held at Google in Silicon Valley the following day. Being a light sleeper, Alex woke up around 2:30 in the morning and saw a woman walking around the room. At first, he thought he was dreaming, and then maybe that it was Jean, but a moment later he realized that his wife was sleeping next to him.

He jumped out of bed and asked the woman who she was and what she was doing there, but she ran out of the room with his wallet and a bracelet that he took off only when he went to sleep. Alex chased her down the hall, but he tore the Achilles tendon in one leg, and in his words, "fell in an ignominious heap to the carpeting." He managed to limp to the lobby, where he told security staff what had happened, and then he headed to the hospital.

Lucinda Moyers had been previously convicted for burglary, and she was arrested and held on $625,000 bail. She said that she didn't know it was Trebek in the room, and when she appeared in court her attorney said she was a prostitute and was actually in the hotel to meet a customer.

Alex didn't care about the stolen money, he just wanted the bracelet back because Lucille had given it to him about ten years earlier. She was out running errands and saw a chunky silver bracelet on the ground near her car. She brought it home and asked her son to take a look. He did some research and discovered that it was a Gucci bracelet that was no longer made and was worth about $800. But to Alex it was much more valuable than that, because it was a gift from his mother.

After the police failed to find the bracelet, he searched for a replacement, and found one at an estate jeweler in New York. He was thrilled, and couldn't wait to tell Jean the news, but when he did she informed him that she'd found a jeweler who could make a duplicate for him. "So I now have two," he said, and sharp-eyed viewers can see that he is never without one of them on the show.

Moyers was later convicted, but it always bugged Alex that the bracelet was never found, so he wrote to Moyers in prison to ask what she had done with it. "She wrote back and apologized, and said she put the bracelet in a trash can on a lower floor, and it's been in the San Francisco dump [ever since]," he said.

A year after the bracelet was stolen, Alex was still having trouble walking as a result of his torn Achilles. His health issues weren't over. Far from it.

He was used to the aches and pains that came from tinkering on projects around the house, so when he started to feel a pain in his back and chest that didn't go away, he wasn't too concerned.

"I've had kidney stones, I've had ruptured discs, so I'm used to dealing with pain," he said, estimating that over his seventy-two years of life he'd had twenty surgeries to deal with wrecked knees and back pain.

But Jean wasn't buying it; she'd long ago learned to keep an eye on her husband's various health issues, since he wasn't about to do it himself, and when she became visibly upset as she urged him to go to the hospital, he finally agreed to go. It's a good thing he did, because the doctors discovered that one of his arteries had become blocked, resulting in a second heart attack.

Alex spent four nights in the hospital before heading home. He briefly pondered easing up on his home-improvement projects and starting to be more careful about his health, but he predicted, "I wouldn't count on it."

After all, he had an exercise room at the house with a treadmill that had rarely been used, and he admitted that it was unlikely he'd change his habits anytime soon. "If I thought [exercise] was really important, I would do it," he said.

Shortly after his second heart attack, *Dancing with the Stars* came calling to invite him on the show, but his physician wasn't crazy about the prospect, even though a follow-up EKG revealed a clean bill of health.

DWTS persisted, but Alex always passed because of lingering issues with his Achilles, not to mention his shaky knees and continuing back problems.

In addition to watching over her husband's health, Jean had been after him to retire from *Jeopardy!* for years. After all, at a rumored yearly salary of $10 million, they didn't need the money. But despite his talking about retirement on and off for years, Alex was reluctant to give up his gig, because he still liked doing it. "Saying that I've *thought* about retiring doesn't mean that I'm *doing* it," he said.

Yet, after twenty-eight years as the host of *Jeopardy!* he—and other people—couldn't help pondering it. "People have been telling me, 'Alex, you've got to go for at least thirty, so at least do two more,'" he said. "[Thirty] has a nice ring to it."

Besides, he added, if he retired he wasn't sure he'd spend his time any differently, given the fact that he worked only two days every two weeks anyway. "I'd be lost," he admitted. "Jean would say I'm getting on her nerves because I'm around all the time."

But it appeared that Alex came closer to leaving than he ever let on after an episode of *Jeopardy! Kids Week*. A parent was unhappy when her daughter lost after playing two rounds of the game because she was in negative numbers, which meant she couldn't proceed to the final round. The girl ran offstage in tears, and in an email to the show's producers, her mother lambasted Alex for not being sensitive to her daughter's feelings and not going backstage to help calm her down.

"If he had taken the time, he would have known that my daughter is not a sore loser, and does not become emotional solely over losing a game," the mother wrote. "She was upset about not being able to completely play the game to the end."

By itself, this was a ludicrous request, given that the show's tight taping schedule meant there was little time to placate a losing contestant, whether adult or adolescent, even if Alex had wanted to. But the mother asked if they could retape the segment. It was a radical request, to be sure, but when one of the producers asked if he would acquiesce, Alex lashed out in an email he dictated to a staffer. "If you all think I should retape the opening, I will, but I want to say that for thirty years I've defended our show against attacks inside and out. But it doesn't seem to operate both ways. When I'm vilified, corporate [and certainly legal] always seems to say, 'Don't say anything and it'll blow over,' and I'm not feeling support from the producers, and that disappoints the shit out of me."

He ended his missive with a thinly veiled threat: "If I'm making mistakes and saying things you don't like, maybe it's time for me to move on."

He later attributed the girl's meltdown to an increasing societal tendency where it had become totally okay for parents to coddle their children, often to extremes. "Our show attracts brighter people and—particularly in regard to children—they don't know how to fail," he said.

While he blamed the parents, he felt sorry for the kids. "They show their emotions very readily and tear up because they wanted to do so much better," he said. "I feel for them."

In fact, he was becoming increasingly outspoken about how he thought American society was moving in the wrong direction, which was especially noticeable when he was in New York, where he frequently took the subway.

"Everyone has their face buried in their cell phones," he said. "There's a lack of civility in our society right now that bothers me, and it frightens me that we're losing sensitivity toward others."

To counteract this trend, he took great pride in sending handwritten letters to both fans and friends. One recent Christmas, he sent a letter to a friend who mailed out holiday newsletters each year. "She wrote me back and said, 'A handwritten letter! I can't tell you how big of an impact it had on me and my family for you to take the time to sit down and write a letter.'"

He zeroed in on the increasing lack of warmth and connection caused by social media, where people feel comfortable with broadcasting the minutiae of their everyday lives. "Why is it important to know what I did this morning and convey that to other people?" he asked.

With 2014 approaching—marking either the thirtieth or fiftieth anniversary of the show's inception, depending on how you looked at it—Alex wanted to both honor and celebrate the show's longevity and strength.

And there were many others who wanted to celebrate with him, including the Smithsonian in Washington, D.C. The esteemed historical organization asked him to donate some of his most treasured keepsakes from the show. He rustled through his files and found his script from the first *Jeopardy!* show he ever hosted, covered with his notes and jottings.

Alex and the staff marked the milestone with a Battle of the Decades, a five-week tournament featuring the five top winners from the 1980s, 1990s, and 2000s. As with other tournament weeks, the ratings enjoyed a bump, but some longtime fans took issue with the fact that the show was not celebrating its *fiftieth* anniversary, since the original version with Art Fleming first aired in 1964.

Executive producer Harry Friedman said that this wasn't a mistake, and that the fact that the show was on hiatus for almost a decade before returning was the reason for the discrepancy. "The lack of continuity makes it feel weird to say it's the fiftieth anniversary," he explained.

Underscoring the occasion, Alex was named the eighth most trusted person in America, based on a poll conducted by *Reader's Digest*; he was in between Bill Gates, at seventh place, and his wife, Melinda Gates, in ninth place. Friedman was not surprised. "Credibility, consistency, integrity, and a real sense that he's completely engaged in the game—that's what defines his appeal," he said.

In fact, the years in the run-up to the thirtieth anniversary were filled with tributes to both Alex and the show. In 2011, he won a Lifetime Achievement Award at the Daytime Emmy Awards—along with Pat Sajak—and in 2012 *Jeopardy!* won its first-ever Peabody Award, a prestigious annual honor to recognize excellence in broadcasting, and a second Emmy in the Outstanding Game/Audience Participation Show category, bringing its total Emmy haul to 30. Alex had been nominated for Outstanding Game Show Host in every year between 1985 and 2011, and had won five times. And a few years later, on June 13, 2014, he set a Guinness World Record for "the most game show episodes hosted by the same presenter": 6,829.

Despite his reluctance to engage in social media—indeed in anything that involved technology—the online community had long embraced Alex and the show. Younger people—particularly college students—had tuned in to the show from the days of Art Fleming. But, as hoped, when the show's writers began to expand into categories that were more contemporary in scope, where the answers consisted of hip-hop and rap lyrics, this demographic's viewership numbers rose—especially when Alex read them aloud. *Jeopardy!* had started to include entire categories on rap and hip-hop in the late 1980s, especially during college tournaments, but perhaps the first time Alex rapped lyrics as clues came during a 2009 College Championship with the category "MC Trebek in Da Hizzouse."

So it was totally understandable that when Alex started to trend on Twitter, on January 6, 2014, millions of *Jeopardy!* fans felt their hearts skip a beat: had Alex *died*? After a few clicks, their worry turned to relief and then laughter as they saw that the previous night's episode had featured him gamely rapping *Jeopardy!* answers in the category "It's a Rap," which included quotes from songs by Run DMC and Dr. Dre. In the first three clues, Alex read the clues in a straightforward manner, but he added a bit of a twangy drawl toward the end. Of course, the clips went viral, and the show's producers and writers took notice for the future.

Head writer Billy Wisse said that while they can't include any lyrics that are past a PG rating, "We try to get some things that sound a little bit goofy coming out of Alex's mouth," just as they had done with foreign pronunciations.

The year 2014 came and went, and still Alex was reluctant to part ways with the show, though he began to hint that he would probably retire at the end of his current contract, which would be up in 2016.

"There are other things I'd like to do," he said. "Traveling more would be nice."

He even went out on a limb and suggested possible replacements to stand behind his podium, including CNN anchor Anderson Cooper. "All of us are replaceable," he said. "While the person who replaces me might not be readily accepted by the viewers initially, in a very short time he or she would win them over."

However, he did step away from some projects. After twenty-five years of hosting the National Geographic Bee, he ended that gig in 2013, and TV journalist Soledad O'Brien stepped in to fill his shoes.

"I'm not going to go on forever. There is a time for all things, and my time might be coming."

His words would turn out to be more prescient than anyone could have predicted.

12

LETTING GO

Early in his career, when queried about his political leanings, Alex never made any secret of his politics bending more conservative than liberal.

But as he aged—and admittedly mellowed—when asked by reporters or audience members which way he leaned, he came firmly out as somewhere squarely in the middle. "I'm an independent," he said. "I'm not ultraconservative, but I'm not ultraliberal either." And while he used to consider himself a regular viewer of Fox News, he said that he had switched to CNN or ABC in recent years.

After five-plus decades in the public spotlight, and increasingly aware of the influence he wielded, Alex started to become more outspoken, not only in his views about politics but also about specific candidates. Leading up to the 2016 presidential election, he hoped the next president would be "somebody like an FDR . . . to inspire people, and not somebody whose negativity will take us all down."

And though he once entertained thoughts of running for

public office, he had since changed his mind. "The amount of [distress] you have to deal with is just beyond belief," he said. "I don't know why people go into politics now—they're either crooked or really dedicated, because you're subject to such vitriol, all kinds of accusations, fair and unfair. Who'd want to do that?"

In 2018, he also rued the fact that politics had supplanted most other subjects as the focus of everyday life for many Americans. "Politics now are like the days of the O. J. Simpson trial—it's all we do every day," he said.

At the same time, he didn't rule out accepting a position in his native Canada, not as prime minister but as governor general, a largely ceremonial job that is appointed by the Queen. "It's a real job, but mostly PR," he said. "You travel the country and make people feel good about themselves, their accomplishments, and the country."

But just as he'd described the prospect of retirement— "When something is important enough to you, you do it, so if I haven't, it's because it wasn't all that important to me"—he eventually ruled out holding any political office, appointed or elected.

But he didn't hesitate to use his visibility and popularity as a soapbox for important topics of the day, which went double when it came to climate change. Deeply incensed, he said, "Ninety-seven percent of the scientists and climatologists of the world agree on this, and yet there are people like [Trump] who say, 'There are scientists who don't agree.'

"Those of you who do not believe in global warming, shut up," he said.

Alex might have been particularly punchy in the summer

of 2016, because aside from the contentious run-up to the 2016 elections, his mom died of a stroke at the age of ninety-five. Alex had frequently talked about the good aging genes that Lucille had passed down to him, and she had been such a fixture in his life—as in his family life—that it came as a shock to him when she was finally gone.

Of course, his own health wasn't getting any better; he'd finally had a full knee replacement in December 2015, which is why he had to sit down while hosting the show for a few months. But just before Christmas 2017 came something far more serious: Alex underwent surgery to remove a subdural hematoma—blood clots—from his brain, caused when he'd taken a serious tumble in autumn. The sizable clots had been pressing against his brain, which had brought on a bout of depression and other symptoms. He'd figured everything was probably due to his bereavement over Lucille's death, but he'd also started to worry that he was showing signs of having had a stroke. "It scared the daylights out of me," he admitted.

He spent two days in the hospital before starting rehab at home. Shortly afterward, he released a video to thank fans for their concern, and told them that he'd be back at work shortly after the New Year.

As every new development went public, talk of Alex's retirement increased. But it was a health scare that went unseen by his fans that caused the most worry for him. Despite his earlier cognitive tests in the wake of not being able to conjure up the word "broccoli," he still worried that he was showing signs of having early Alzheimer's disease. He was regularly making errors, like reversing numbers—referring to the year 1942 when he was clearly thinking of 1492—and getting the right answer for a crossword puzzle but squeezing the word into the wrong space. He was tested again, more rigorously—after all, he'd be celebrating his eightieth birthday in a few years—and was relieved that he tested negative again, and that his slipups were the result of natural cognitive decline caused by aging. He said he'd hold on to his job for the time being, but added, "When it's clear that it's time for me to go, I'll go."

Besides, he still maintained a scrap of vanity. "I don't have the kind of ego that would drive me to be wheeled onstage," he said.

Mindful of the brouhaha that had erupted when he decided to shave his mustache back in 2001—and because people never quite stopped asking him about it—Alex decided to have a little fun. When the show returned from hiatus in the fall of 2018 for its thirty-fifth season, he was again sporting facial hair.

Only this time, it didn't involve a mustache, but a full beard. "I decided to regrow my mustache, but as you can see things got a little out of hand—hairs kept attracting friends," he told the studio audience.

He then threw down the gauntlet, telling viewers that the decision on whether he should pick up a razor was theirs to make, and that they could cast their vote on the *Jeopardy!* Instagram account with an #AlexTrebeard hashtag.

The internet, understandably, went nuts. After the dust settled, the final vote was pro-beard, 73 to 27 percent, with just over eighteen thousand votes cast. But a clean-shaven Alex walked onto the set a week later and broke the news to fans that in the end, their votes didn't count after all: Jean had veto power, and she didn't like the beard, so off it came.

That season also held other surprises, including when the drag queen RuPaul appeared on *Jeopardy!* to present the clues in a category with the title of "A RuView of Movies," about drag in movies. During the segment, Alex revealed he was going to appear in a guest spot on *RuPaul's Drag Race* where he gave the clue "What is chunky, yet funky?" He punctuated "funky" with a slight twist of his torso, hands on hips, a reference to the zaftig Latrice Royale, who had appeared on the fourth season of *Drag Race*.

In the fall of 2018, he branched out yet again, serving as moderator in the Pennsylvania gubernatorial debate. Though both politicians and voters looked forward to his appearance in the forty-five-minute debate between the Democratic incumbent Tom Wolf and his Republican challenger, Scott Wagner, Alex flubbed his role as moderator from the get-go. Instead of asking the two candidates questions and keeping track of their allotted time to answer, he seemed to view it as a kind of speaking engagement. He offered meandering observations about how when he was a boy at Catholic school, none of the priests were molesting students, along with the fact that the California state legislature had one lawmaker for every 325,000 residents, even though his rambling statements had nothing to do with Pennsylvania.

Afterward, he was soundly criticized by local media as well as the candidates, and later he offered up a mea culpa, saying that he had presented a few ideas to shake up the traditional debate formula. But in the aftermath, he admitted that he should have anticipated the backlash. "What on earth was I thinking?" he said.

The joy of celebrating the show's thirty-fifth year overshadowed everything, and the accolades that came forth clearly underscored what a rarity it was for a game show to achieve that benchmark. "What Harry Friedman and the team has had is the ability to take a very simple format and slightly change it and tweak it and enhance it over the years," said Mike Hopkins, chairman of Sony Pictures Television. "To move forward without stripping away the essence is pretty remarkable for a thirty-five-year-old show."

"It's reassuring for people to know, 'This is the show I used to watch, or my mom used to watch, or my grandmother used to watch,'" said Ken Jennings.

As 2019 got under way, Alex continued with his usual schedule of taping shows, traveling, and thinking up new ways he could help people, both by using his time and allocating funds through the foundation. He felt the typical aches and pains of being in his eighth decade—whether or not they were caused by falling off a ladder—but one day he realized he was having stomach pain that wasn't going away.

Usually he chalked it up to indigestion and it cleared up in a few days. But this time the pain didn't recede, and in fact, it got worse. Jean urged him to go to the doctor, who conducted a series of tests, and it soon became clear that the cause of his stomach pain wouldn't be eased by medication or surgery. The doctor told Alex that he had "a bulge in his stomach the size of a small fist." He had stage 4 pancreatic cancer, which meant it had already started to spread to other parts of his body.

Alex and Jean were in shock. They took some time to process the information, told their family and a few close friends—and then Alex told the world.

Fans who had set their online alerts for *Jeopardy!* news probably thought that when they received the text on March 6, 2019, Alex had posted a video for viewers to weigh in on whether he should grow another mustache, or maybe that he'd set the date for the next Tournament of Champions. Instead they were stunned when he revealed that he had been recently diagnosed with stage 4 pancreatic cancer, one of the deadliest cancers out there, with a 25 percent survival rate just a year past the initial diagnosis, and only a 3 percent chance of surviving to five years.

Surprisingly, he didn't appear depressed, but slightly upbeat, as he confided to viewers that he wanted to be the one to tell it to them straight, and didn't want them to learn about it via some sensationalized tabloid story. "I wanted our viewers to get the facts straight from the horse's mouth," he said.

"Like fifty thousand other people in the United States each year, this week I was diagnosed with stage 4 pancreatic cancer," he said, telling millions of fans that he vowed to fight as hard as he could, even joking that he had no choice in the matter, since he owed three more years on his *Jeopardy!* contract.

The video lasted only seventy-three seconds, but both its impact and the resulting reaction were swift, with celebrities weighing in and fans offering their prayers . . . and astonishment.

"Trebek seems eternal; he's one of TV's archetypal father figures in the way he chats with contestants like a father standing on the porch with a prom date: dutiful, genial, stilted," wrote Sam Anderson, a staff writer with *The New York Times Magazine*, admitting that the diagnosis "almost didn't make sense. It was like the Grand Canyon getting leukemia."

ABC News correspondent Chris Connelly concurred. "He's always been like the Empire State Building, something you can always count on in a time of great change," he said. "For him to express a kind of vulnerability has really touched a lot of people."

Despite the devastating news, Alex maintained his regular schedule, taping new episodes of *Jeopardy!*, traveling, spending time with his family, and making the rounds of the national talk-show circuit, all the while embarking on a rigorous program of chemotherapy. Some days he felt fine, but on others he felt as if he'd been hit by a truck.

In the few days after chemo, when he had to be on the set of *Jeopardy!*, Alex found that first his vision blurred, and then his bones and joints started to hurt. It also affected his performance on the game. "I could still deliver the clues at a rapid pace, but I seemed a little slower in the ad-lib portions," he said.

On the bad days, instead of chatting with the makeup artist during a touch-up or joking around with his wardrobe guy during breaks, he was curled up on the floor of his dressing room, crying from the stabbing pain.

His worried staff would tell him it was no problem to shut down production for the day, but Alex refused. "No, we're here," he'd respond, "we're doing the shows," though when the pain got particularly excruciating, he'd ask staffers if they had anything he could take to blunt it.

In other words, "The show must go on." According to Alex, "I can always suck it up when it comes time to tape the show."

His only concession to the cancer was that he started to wear a wig on camera after losing his hair from chemo; most viewers never noticed. In fact, he later joked that the wig was a big improvement on his original hair. He also could no longer taste his food—the chemo had wreaked havoc on his sense of taste.

But he was absolutely blown away by the letters and gifts he received from fans from all over the world. "Prayers have been said on my behalf," he told people. "I've received holy oil from the Padre Pio congregation and holy water from Lourdes, and also a lot of cannabis from well-wishers."

In the middle of his cancer treatment, seemingly out of no-where, came a contestant whose reign would quickly prove to rival the prodigious talent—and winnings of Ken Jennings.

James Holzhauer, from Naperville, Illinois, made his first appearance as a contestant on April 4, 2019. For much of his childhood, he had watched the show with his grandmother, who was from Japan and far from fluent in English, and when he was still a child, he vowed that one day he would appear on the show. The first time he tried out was in 2006, the initial year of online testing, but he didn't make it, though he con-tinued to take the test once a year.

It wasn't until 2012 that he really buckled down in his pur-suit of gaining a spot on the show. His strategy? Reading as many children's books as he could get his hands on and, as he put it, "learning at least the basics of every subject I could imagine popping up on the show," adding that children's books are ideal for *Jeopardy!* study, because they focus on the building blocks and essential facts of any given topic.

He won $43,680 on his first day, and topped that by winning $110,914 on his fourth appearance, making history as having won the most money in one day on the show. By the end of his thirty-third game, he'd won $2,464,216, about $58,000 short of Ken Jennings's total winnings in 2004. Holzhauer was a professional gambler by trade, and the reason he broke so many records was a combination of his making huge bets—he felt he was playing with house money, since it didn't come out of his own pocket—and his favoring the Forrest Bounce, the technique that Alex frowned on—jumping around the board and picking the highest-value clues first. And, of course, he was lightning-fast when it came to hitting the buzzer.

Alex, who received his cancer diagnosis during Holzhauer's run, was in awe of his star player. "His knowledge is so broad," he said. "There are moments in the games when I'm thinking, 'How the hell did he know that?'"

But producers must have been concerned that even though the ratings had exploded since Holzhauer had started his run, his almost-daily record-breaking wins were stressing their prize-money coffers.

"Every game show has a prize budget," said Bob Boden, who had previously programmed shows at Game Show Network. "Typically, for a long-running show the prize budget is determined by way of averages of what has been won in the past. James's performance, I'm sure, [was] causing grief for an accountant somewhere."

Just a couple of months after making his announcement about the cancer, Alex had some good news for worried fans, telling them that some of the tumors had shrunk considerably and that his doctors were ecstatic about what he called a "near remission." The next phase of treatment involved immunotherapy, which boosts the body's immune system in order to fight the disease.

His doctors were astounded, but Alex took the news in stride. He firmly believed that the overwhelming response from people around the world was partially responsible for the cancer easing. "This has to be more than just chemo," he said. "I've had a couple million people out there who have expressed their good thoughts, their positive energy, and their prayers."

But he confided that the fight hadn't been easy. "I've discovered that I'm a bit of a wuss, but I'm fighting through it," he said.

When taping for the thirty-fifth season ended shortly after his hopeful announcement, fans contented themselves with watching reruns and trusting that Alex would be cancer-free by the time the new season commenced in the fall. At the end of August 2019, to welcome fans to Season 36 in the fall, Alex posted his usual video. "We have some exciting things coming up," he said, "and I can't wait to share them with all of you. Let me tell you, it's going to be a good year."

But fans were taken aback at the radical change in his appearance in just a few months. He looked tired and sallow, his weight loss was visible—one week he lost a whopping twelve pounds—and his diction was not as crisp as usual, though he was his normal upbeat self. In the eighty-second video, he confided that instead of his rebounding, the cancer had returned with a vengeance and he'd had to undergo more chemotherapy over the summer. "The immunotherapy didn't do diddly-squat," he said.

He confided that the treatment and the side effects and the illness were taking their toll. "I leave home and I'm in terrible shape sometimes," he said.

Which he attributed to the unpredictable nature of both the cancer and the treatment. "I never know from one day to the next because, if it isn't the chemotherapy, it's the disease itself that is affecting me," he said. "I'll be feeling fine for half the day and all of a sudden a tremendous depression descends or I'll suddenly start experiencing pain where I didn't have it five minutes ago. And the pain moves."

But he refused to cancel or postpone tapings, because something magical still happened once he arrived at the studio and was dressed and primped to prepare for the cameras and contestants. "The adrenaline kicks in and I go out onstage and it seems to work," he said, though he struggled through the fatigue, nausea, and excruciating pain.

He was particularly bothered by the effect that the chemo had on his speaking abilities. "I'm slurring my words and my tongue doesn't work as well as it used to, since the chemo has caused sores inside my mouth, which makes it difficult for me to speak and enunciate properly," he admitted. While show staff said they didn't see much of a difference, Alex did, and that's what mattered, in addition to his worry about viewers who might be aware of the changes.

Jean, Matt, and Emily tried to support him as best they could, but one of their concerns was that despite his openness with reporters and the public about the cancer, he was holding his cards too close to his chest when it came to them.

"They're not quite certain that it's exactly as I am portraying it, because I don't communicate that much," he said.

He admitted that Jean had a difficult job when it came to taking care of him. "It's always tough for caretakers," he said. "I'm not always the most pleasant person to be around when I'm experiencing severe pain or depression."

While she tried to remain her regular upbeat self, and frequently called upon her spiritual faith, Jean openly admitted she was severely tested whenever her husband was clearly struggling, the worst part being when Alex is "in pain and I can't help him."

Both Emily and Matthew were busy with their own professional lives, but they visited their father as often as they could. The family was still extremely close and still traveled together whenever possible. In September 2019, Alex and Jean went to England to retrace their steps in their shared love of everything *Wuthering Heights*. They were visiting the Brontë Parsonage in West Yorkshire when Jean turned around to see Matthew and Emily walking toward them, to celebrate her birthday.

When Jean started to cry, they all teared up, and Alex was reminded of how far he had traveled from his days of living as an isolated bachelor to his now being a contented and fulfilled father and husband. For Alex, the trip was marred by his extreme frailty: they couldn't wander through the moors they so loved, and it was a real struggle to walk around the Brontë Parsonage. Still, he was thrilled that he was able to make the trip and spend time with his beloved family.

The occasion also reminded him of another worry. "It bothers me that I might pass on before I get to have a grandchild," he confided.

But there was one thing he was absolutely clear about. Whenever someone asked why he was still doing the show—why, with such an uncertain future ahead of him, he wasn't checking things off his bucket list and spending what might be the very little time he had left with his family—he became a bit defensive. "This is my job, my life," he said. "My whole career has been in television, hosting programs. Why wouldn't I want to continue to do this as long as I can?"

And despite years of telling her husband that he should kick back a bit and go ahead and give retirement a try, even Jean had come around. "I know it's what feeds him," she said. "He loves doing *Jeopardy!* He has his own family over there; they're such a close-knit, beautiful group of people."

But it became clear that reality was sinking in when Alex and Jean put their beloved lake house in Paso Robles up for sale in the spring 2019. "Our home was becoming more of an obligation than an inspiration," said Jean. "'Bittersweet' is the perfect word to describe the feeling I have about the sale of our home."

The house sold in late summer.

•   •   •

Throughout the fall of 2019, the online posts and letters and prayers continued to pour in; there was never any doubt about how viewers and contestants felt about Alex. But on the program that aired on November 11, 2019, one contestant took it a step further.

Contestant Dhruv Gaur was down to $2,000, but he couldn't stop thinking about how Alex was struggling; the show was taped in mid-September, a couple of weeks after Alex announced that he had resumed chemotherapy. "We were all hurting for him so badly," Dhruv explained.

The Final Jeopardy! category was "Famous Phrases," with the answer: "In the title of a groundbreaking 1890 exposé of poverty in New York City slums, these 3 words follow 'How the.'"

The correct question was "Other Half Lives," based on the 1890 book by Jacob Riis, a photojournalist who captured the squalid lives of the millions of New Yorkers living in slums and working in sweatshops.

Dhruv initially drew a blank. "I could've tried to puzzle it together," he said, "but really, I just kept thinking about Alex."

When Alex called on him, he was wearing a grin a mile wide. "Dhruv, you're smiling—I like that. Let's take a look at your response," Alex said. "Did you come up with the right one? No. What is, 'We love you Alex.'" He paused before he continued in a choked-up voice, "That's very kind of you; thank you."

Dhruv had bet $1,995, which left him with just $5, but that didn't really matter, because the internet went nuts.

The next day Dhruv shared on Twitter that he was "really

glad I got the opportunity to say to Alex what everybody at the tournament was thinking."

As 2019 progressed and fans and media latched onto every episode, media interview, or tabloid headline for news of his disease, Alex, ever the host and not the star, confided that he felt uncomfortable about being the focus of attention, and pondered that maybe he should have kept his cards close to the vest after all.

"There are moments when I regret going public with it, because there's a little too much of Alex Trebek out there right now," he said.

At times, he also wasn't thrilled with the fact that he'd become the unofficial spokesperson for pancreatic cancer. In addition to dealing with the ups and downs of his own disease, his natural empathy and affinity for other people meant that he couldn't help getting drawn into what complete strangers were dealing with in their own battles. He took pride in being able to be a role model for others, but he admitted, "It does place a responsibility on me that I feel I'm not deserving of."

He had started to correspond with a woman who was struggling with her own recent diagnosis of pancreatic cancer, and it clearly took a toll on him. "I tried to cheer her up as best I could, but it's tough sometimes trying to be as optimistic as you can when the other person feels none of that optimism," he said. "I don't know if I'm strong enough or intelligent enough to help alleviate some of that despair, so it's tough on me."

But he acknowledged that his cancer had helped him grow. "Throughout my life I've always wondered how courageous a human being I was," he said. "[Am] I courageous for dealing with [the cancer]? No. I could be scared to death and I'd still have to deal with it. But I'm not scared to death, so maybe I am courageous."

In early 2020, he continued to tape *Jeopardy!* episodes and give interviews to talk-show hosts about his life and his future. Whereas he had remained upbeat and optimistic over most of the first year of his diagnosis, as he passed the first anniversary Alex had become increasingly pragmatic and realistic about his odds of survival. "I'm nearing the end of life, I know that," he said. "I'm not gonna delude myself."

On the whole, however, he said he was stunned at the flood of correspondence he'd received since his diagnosis. "[It's] humbled me, really," he said. "I had no idea that our show and myself had such an impact on the lives of so many people out there."

He added, "Most people don't get to see this because it happens after they're gone. But *I* get to see it."

But others weren't surprised in the least over the outpouring of love for him. "Alex is always there," said Ken Jennings. "It's so assuring to have his voice in your ear for half an hour every night, no matter how your day was. He's got it under control, and we need that."

Of course, aside from *Jeopardy!* reruns, he won't always be there, but Alex said that even though he's close to the end of his life, he has absolutely no regrets. "My life has been a quest for knowledge and understanding," he said. "I will die without having come up with the answers to many things in life, and it doesn't bother me in the least."

And after living with terminal cancer, he's made his peace with fate. "I'm not afraid of dying. One thing they're not going to say at my funeral is 'He was taken from us too soon,'" he said.

"If there's one thing I have discovered in the past year, it is the power of prayer. I learned it from the Jesuits when I was a kid," he said.

Naturally, talk turned to the question of who would replace such a beloved, iconic, seemingly irreplaceable host. Alex himself had mentioned a few possibilities through the years, occasionally in jest.

"It's probably going to be a woman, somebody younger, somebody bright, somebody personable, somebody with a great sense of humor," he said. "I nominated Betty White." Alex floated a few more ideas, including CNN analyst Laura Coates; Alex Faust, an announcer with the LA Kings hockey team; and TCM host Ben Mankiewicz. "There are so many talented people out there that could do the job."

Some have suggested Ken Jennings, especially since he won the Greatest of All Time Tournament in January 2020. And while he said that he'd definitely consider it, Jennings couldn't allow himself to go there yet. "It's a great job, but that would mean Alex isn't hosting the show, and I'm not emotionally prepared for that," he said.

Alex also speculated openly about his last day on the set. He'd like to leave the show in the same manner as he shaved off his mustache back in 2001: on the spur of the moment.

"I'll do it on a whim," he said. The day he makes his decision, he'll tell executive producer Harry Friedman and director Clay Jacobsen to schedule the show so there are thirty extra seconds at the end. "I will say, 'Until we meet again, God bless you and goodbye.'"

ACKNOWLEDGMENTS

Eternal thanks go to Superagent, aka Scott Mendel, as well as to everyone at St. Martin's Press and Thomas Dunne Books, including Tom Dunne, Sally Richardson, Stephen S. Power, Lisa Bonvissuto, John Karle, Mary Moates, and Sara Beth Haring. And kudos to copy editor Thomas Cherwin.

NOTES

INTRODUCTION

1 "He just seems sort of immortal": Jonah Engel Bromwich, "Why America Loves Alex Trebek." *New York Times*, March 8, 2019.

1 "get him some French fries or something": Noreen Malone, "The Last King of the American Middlebrow." *New Republic*, May 26, 2014.

2 "turning *Jeopardy!* on is always kind of a grounding experience": Jonah Engel Bromwich, "Why America Loves Alex Trebek." *New York Times*, March 8, 2019.

2 "I just keep on going": Daniel Stone, "Is Alex Trebek in Jeopardy?" *Newsweek*, February 21, 2011.

3 "I'm curious about everything, even things that don't interest me": A. J. Jacobs, *The Know-It-All*. New York: Simon & Schuster, 2004.

3 "I love acquiring knowledge, even useless knowledge": Barrie Nedler, Interview. Television Academy Foundation, August 22, 2007.

3 "the good things that have happened to me have happened by

accident": "Who is Alex Trebek? Celebrating 35 Seasons of *Jeopardy!*" 92Y Talk with Michael McKean, February 19, 2019.

3 "if someone offers you something, you accept it": Doug Krikorian, "Celebrity Race Is Not in *Jeopardy!*" *Press-Telegram*, April 9, 2009.

3 "since I'm always trying to better myself": Jeanne Wolf, "Three Questions: Alex Trebek." *Saturday Evening Post*, January/February 2016.

3 "I wish I could stop and smell the roses": Cheryl Lavin, "Vital Statistics: Alex Trebek": *Chicago Tribune*, January 24, 1988.

4 "game shows were the beginning and best of reality television": William Keck, "Keck's Exclusives: Alex Trebek on Retiring from *Jeopardy* and His Possible Successor." *TV Guide*, May 9, 2013.

4 "without feeling you have to flee the room to go watch your own show": Barrie Nedler, Interview. Television Academy Foundation, August 22, 2007.

4 "and doing that has allowed me to develop as a human": David Marchese, "In Conversation: Alex Trebek." *Vulture*, November 19, 2018.

5 "I didn't want to make any mistakes": *The Howard Stern Show*, May 11, 2015.

5 "This is part of his charm": Sam Anderson, "How Watching *Jeopardy!* Together Helped Me Say Goodbye to My Father." *New York Times Magazine*, December 8, 2019.

5 "and I'm not emotionally prepared for that": Jacob Uitti, "Ken Jennings Talks Strategy, Marvel Movies, and Alex Trebek." Interview.com, February 10, 2020.

6 "such an impact on the lives of so many people out there": "Channel 11's Jennifer Tomazic Sits Down with *Jeopardy!* Host Alex Trebek." WPXI-TV, February 10, 2020.

6 "and to lend proper perspective in difficult situations": "Alex Trebek." Success Talk with Peter Lowe, 1997.

6 "and found so many worthwhile things along the way": Ibid.

1. PILOT, DOCTOR, OR PRIME MINISTER?

8 "It was new": Robert Edelstein, "Alex Trebek." *Broadcasting & Cable*, October 28, 2013.

8 "I fell in love with Hollywood and show business": "Who is Alex Trebek? Celebrating 35 Seasons of *Jeopardy!*" 92Y Talk with Michael McKean, February 19, 2019.

10 "My dad got along with everybody": Barrie Nedler, Interview. Television Academy Foundation, August 22, 2007.

10 "Those afternoon gatherings got to be pretty lively": Alex Trebek Talk, Ukrainian Culture Center, Los Angeles, August 21, 2011.

11 "she would whack me pretty hard sometimes": Harvey Levin, *OBJECTified*. Fox News, July 29, 2018.

11 "I just couldn't wait to get to the next page": Jeanne Wolf, "Three Questions: Alex Trebek." *Saturday Evening Post*, January/February 2016.

11 "the two combined to make a loner": Alan Ebert, "We Visit with Alex Trebek." *Good Housekeeping*, August 1992.

11 "He'd sit on the steps and watch the other children play": Margot Dougherty, "Sorry, Girls, Mom Keeps House for *Jeopardy!* Host Alex Trebek." *People*, October 12, 1987.

11 "it might be what inspired my love of reading": "Celebrities Share with PARADE: 'The Book That Changed My Life.'" *Parade*, June 8, 2012.

12 "It had everything a young boy would be fascinated in": Harry Wilson, "Alex Trebek." *Canadian Geographic*, April 2015.

12 "I made it a point to go to a lot of doctor and dentist appointments": Melody Kramer, "Alex Trebek: On Hosting the National Geographic Bee." *National Geographic*, May 21, 2013.

13 "I got whacked by the nuns for throwing snowballs and bothering the girls": "One on One with Markus—Alex Trebek." CBC News, November 28, 2017.

13 "We couldn't imagine anything more fantastic": Stephen Cole, "7 Questions with Alex Trebek." *Globe and Mail*, June 2, 2006.

13 "you can be anything you want to be": *Game Changers*, Ammo Content. DVD, 2018.

14 "I've never thrown anything away": Harvey Levin, *OBJECTified*. Fox News, July 29, 2018.

15 "It was a great way to start my career": Chris Taylor, "*Jeopardy!* Host Alex Trebek Provides a Few Answers of His Own." Reuters, March 23, 2017.

15 "I was one of the more difficult students in class": Harvey Levin, *OBJECTified*. Fox News, July 29, 2018.

16 "and I was determined to do the same [to him]": Bert Hill, "TV Host Praises U of O: Alex Trebek Tells Graduates Success Takes Time." *Ottawa Citizen*, June 9, 1997.

16 "I didn't steal the keys, I *found* them": *All in a Day*. CBC, May 3, 2016.

17 "you do well in class, you get privileges": "Alex Trebek," *Rockburn Presents*. CPAC, July 11, 2013.

17 "the diary consisted of nothing but the titles of movies I had seen": Barrie Nedler, Interview. Television Academy Foundation, August 22, 2007.

17 "They thought I was the epitome of common sense": Cheryl Lavin, "Vital Statistics: Alex Trebek." *Chicago Tribune*, January 24, 1988.

18 "I never really made plans as to what my future would be in terms of an adult": David Baber, "Television Game Show Hosts: Biographies of 32 Stars." Jefferson, North Carolina: McFarland & Company, 2009.

18 "He told me never to lose my love of life": Cheryl Lavin, "Vital Statistics: Alex Trebek." *Chicago Tribune*, January 24, 1988.

20 "Father Labbe taught me about the finer things in life, like good cognac and a fine Cuban cigar": Bert Hill, "TV Host Praises U of O: Alex Trebek Tells Graduates Success Takes Time." *Ottawa Citizen*, June 9, 1997.

20 "and drink a gallon of lemonade because I was so thirsty": John Kiesewetter, "Trebek: Warm Memories of Cincy." *Cincinnati Enquirer*, September 16, 2012.

21 "What better way than through religion?" Kit Boss, "Category: Game Shows. Answer: A Real Know-It-All." *Seattle Times*, November 30, 1990.

21 "I was not really into it the way I should have been": Linda Shrieves, "Alex Trebek's Life of *Jeopardy!* Suits the Quiz-Show Host Just Fine." *Dallas Morning News*, December 9, 1992.

22 "I can take an order without you behaving like a jerk": A. J. Jacobs, "What I've Learned." *Esquire*, April 2003.

22 "The thought of being away from her for this extended period of time [didn't help]": Harvey Levin, *OBJECTified*. Fox News, July 29, 2018.

22 "Canadians can do other things than play hockey": Robert Strauss, "Alex Trebek Puts Knee in Jeopardy for Youth Hockey." *Philadelphia Daily News*, February 19, 1988.

23 "I got hit by a car on the way home, but there was no damage to the car": "Alex Trebek," *Rockburn Presents*. CPAC, July 11, 2013.

24 "we wouldn't feel right hiring somebody with absolutely no experience": QTV with Jian Ghomeshi, CBC, June 23, 2008.

25 "all I had to do was take flying lessons": Barrie Nedler, Interview. Television Academy Foundation, August 22, 2007.

2: REACHING FOR THE TOP

27 "I didn't have a chance to get bored with the regular staff announcing tasks": Barrie Nedler, Interview. Television Academy Foundation, August 22, 2007.

29 "to a heavily made-up chap portraying a chunky Jane Tarzan": Andrew Webster, "Televiews." *Ottawa Citizen*, February 22, 1962.

29 "trying to find an answer in life for some things I had seen": Michael Sauter and Melissa Pierson, "The Week." *Entertainment Weekly*. December 22, 1995.

29 "and gets into trouble as a result": Ibid.

30 "It was paradise": QTV with Jian Ghomeshi, CBC, June 23, 2008.

31 "I decided that I should start getting to bed before one o'clock in the morning": *Late Night with David Letterman*, August 15, 1994.

32 "I just had to live with it": *All in a Day*. CBC, May 3, 2016.

32 "Whatever it is, here's somebody to sing it": Knowlton Nash, *Cue the Elephant*. Toronto: McClelland & Stewart, 1996.

32 "feeling the future of the world isn't that bleak after all": Bob Gardiner, "Televiews." *Ottawa Citizen*, October 18, 1963.

33 "For the first time in my life, the show made me enjoy commercials": Sandy Gardiner, "Television." *Ottawa Journal*, May 22, 1964.

33 "the CBC had a responsibility to our listeners to keep them informed": Dean R. Owen, *November 22, 1963: Reflections on the Life, Assassination and Legacy of John F. Kennedy*. New York: Skyhorse Publishing, 2015.

34 "it's not just a question of luck": QTV with Jian Ghomeshi, CBC, June 23, 2008.

34 "what I would wind up doing many, many years later": *All in a Day*. CBC, May 3, 2016.

34 "I was genuinely frightened": Geoff Pevere and Greig Dymond, *Mondo Canuck*. Prentice Hall Canada, 1996.

35 "because you needed it to eat the haggis": Knowlton Nash, *Cue the Elephant*. Toronto: McClelland & Stewart, 1996.

35 "at one time replacing every announcer in every possible job": "Alex Trebek Hosted So Many CBC Shows Before *Jeopardy!*" CBC Archives, July 22, 2018.

37 "cigarette in one hand and paintbrush in the other, and paint the house." "Who Is Alex Trebek? Part I." *A Lot to Learn with Austin Rogers*, October 17, 2019.

37 "the other end never stuck out beyond the rear bumper": Ibid.

38 "get them talking, and give them some good booze": Larry Keller and Christian Millman, and the editors of *Men's Health* Books, *Guy Knowledge*. Emmaus, Pennsylvania: Rodale Press, Inc. 1999.

38 "Any girl who dates me has time for two dates on the same night": Edna Hampton, "Trebek: Cautious, Eligible and Ambitious." *Globe and Mail*, November 25, 1972.

38 "It was an infatuation for each of us, but not destined to survive": Harvey Levin, *OBJECTified*. Fox News, July 29, 2018.

38 "probably good looking": George Maksian, "Alex Trebek: New Canadian Import." *New York Sunday News*, February 24, 1974.

38 "'Boy, look at the knockers on that girl'": Harvey Levin, *OBJECTified*. Fox News, July 29, 2018.

39 "He never gave you the feeling that he wanted you to come up and talk to him": Knowlton Nash, *Cue the Elephant*. Toronto: McClelland & Stewart, 1996.

39 "Alex didn't have to because he never ordered anything": Ibid.

39 "he's extremely intelligent and was destined for success": Ibid.

40 "'Why would Alex have anything like this on the wall?' So I stole it." Knowlton Nash, *Cue the Elephant*. Toronto: McClelland & Stewart, 1996.

40 "no performer is big or important enough to be in command of his show": Alex Barris, *The Pierce-Arrow Showroom Is Leaking*. Toronto: Ryerson Press, 1969.

41 "and somewhat negative about the whole show": Ibid.

42 "and thus be more like his competitors on commercial stations": Blaik Kirby, "More News CBC Aim for Morning Radio." *Globe and Mail*, October 7, 1972.

42 "in search of an audience that isn't there anymore": Ibid.

42 "with a few pleasant words from Trebek to separate them": Ibid.

44 "It's good for your ego": Edna Hampton, "Trebek: Cautious, Eligible and Ambitious." *Globe and Mail*, November 25, 1972.

44 "They don't really know what they're doing": Ibid.

44 "the public attitude suggests that you don't arrive until you've left": Alex Barris, *The Pierce-Arrow Showroom Is Leaking*. Toronto: Ryerson Press, 1969.

45 "than if they're from, say, Australia or Chicago": Ibid.

3: CALIFORNIA, HERE I COME

46 "people said, 'Oh, you're Canadian, you're automatically a nice person'": *Being Canadian*, GRAINEY Pictures, 2015.

47 "memorizing all the details necessary to keep the show moving": "Good Memory Comes in Handy for *Wizard* Emcee." *Daily News-Post*, Monrovia, California, July 28, 1973.

47 "We think that's what women want to see": Norman Mark, "Game Show Host Starts with Good Teeth." *Detroit Free Press*, June 11, 1975.

48 "In fact, I felt this way the first time I visited": Karre Marino, "Alex Trebek Found Life's Answer in LA." *St. Louis Post–Dispatch*, June 8, 1992.

48 "How do you feel about your mustache?": Barrie Nedler, Interview. Television Academy Foundation, August 22, 2007.

49 "Very strongly": Ibid.

49 "I wasn't burning all my bridges": Knowlton Nash, *Cue the Elephant*. Toronto: McClelland & Stewart, 1996.

50 "[Alex] was the tidy one": Kate Hahn, "Alex Trebek to Guest Star on *How I Met Your Mother.*" *TV Guide*, November 17, 2010.

50 "'How many times a day does the average American husband kiss his wife?'": Canadian TV Star Alex Trebek Will Make American TV Debut When NBC's Daytime Game Show *Wizard of Odds* Premieres." Press release, NBC-TV, July 10, 1973.

51 "Don't give the car away": Barrie Nedler, Interview. Television Academy Foundation, August 22, 2007.

52 "Surely before long his embarrassment will show through": Blaik Kirby, "Cable TV Starts Dropping Buffalo Station's Commercials." *Globe and Mail*, July 20, 1973.

53 "actually I was just able to memorize a lot of stuff": Knowlton Nash, *Cue the Elephant*. Toronto: McClelland & Stewart, 1996.

53 "getting away from questions like 'What percentage of men in the country wear undershirts?'": George Maksian, "Alex Trebek: New Canadian Import." *New York Sunday News*, February 24, 1974.

53 "I was a shy, small-town Canadian kid": David Marchese, "In Conversation: Alex Trebek." *Vulture*, November 19, 2018.

54 "I never felt like I belonged": Ibid.

54 "He often needed single guys to fill out the table": Ibid.

55 "I inhaled, and it burned my nose": *The Howard Stern Show*, May 11, 2015.

55 "They put me to bed Friday night because I was almost co-matose": Ibid.

56 "I looked at the blonde lady sitting next to him and said, 'Good-looking companion'": "Who Is Alex Trebek? Part I." *A Lot to Learn with Austin Rogers*, October 17, 2019.

58 "almost every couple on that trip barely made it through still speaking to each other": Peter Marshall and Adrienne Armstrong, *Backstage with the Original Hollywood Square*. Nashville: Rutledge Hill Press, 2002.

58–59 "Her concept of a good show was a good set with an em-cee in an open shirt": Ibid.

59 "But I didn't have to do anything quite that drastic": Clarence Metcalfe, "Remarkable Memory Earns Stardom." *Ottawa Journal*, February 8, 1975.

59 "nor were we willing to compromise": Alan Ebert, "We Visit with Alex Trebek." *Good Housekeeping*, August 1992.

59 "And now I'm one of them": Barrie Nedler, Interview. Television Academy Foundation, August 22, 2007.

4: A VERY DEPRESSED MONK

61 "It was too tough for the room": QTV with Jian Ghomeshi, CBC, June 23, 2008.

61 "have a real good time and get paid for it": Barrie Nedler, Interview. Television Academy Foundation, August 22, 2007.

62 "Otherwise you'll have difficulty keeping things in proper perspective": "Game Shows Are Fun." *News-Journal*, August 4, 1979.

62 "you never know when the next job is going to come up": Barrie Nedler, Interview. Television Academy Foundation, August 22, 2007.

62 "if I like the work, I accept it": Ibid.

63 "didn't have a dime": Alan Ebert, "We Visit with Alex Trebek." *Good Housekeeping*, August 1992.

63 "most important thing a man can fail at, except for fatherhood": Ibid.

64 "It was the worst time of my life": Ibid.

64 "Like a very depressed monk." Ibid.

64 "I spent a lot of evenings that way": "A CTV Portrait of Alex Trebek." CTV Television, December 7, 1996.

68 "Give me a check, please": Alex Trebek, *The Dan Patrick Show*, August 8, 2014.

5: FINALLY . . . *JEOPARDY!*

70 "I am a thick blotter of mostly useless information": Franz Lidz, "What Is *Jeopardy!*?" *Sports Illustrated*, May 1, 1989.

71 "By the time we landed, we had an idea for a show": Ken Jennings, "Buzzed." *Smithsonian*, March 2014.

71 "Then they said, 'There are no jeopardies'": "Interviews with Merv Griffin, Cindy Adams." CNN *Larry King Weekend*, March 15, 2003.

71 "and that's how it got its name": Ibid.

72 *"We're in trouble, yes indeed, We are all in Jeopardy!"*: Jessica Learish and Aaron Pruner, "Secrets of 'Jeopardy!' That Only Superfans Know." Idaily.com, June 26, 2019.

74 "they didn't like anyone messing with its basic structure": Merv Griffin, *Making the Good Life Last*. New York: Simon & Schuster, 2003.

75 "and they still remember the show": Dan McLean, "'Jeopardy' Looks for the Perfect Questions on Visit to San Diego." *Los Angeles Times*, September 12, 1984.

75 "fastest-selling syndicated show": Ibid.

77 "no bright lights, no wild and crazy music": "Alex Trebek Still Has the Answers." *Sudbury Star*, November 7, 2003.

78 "We do not give our winners a year's supply of macaroni": John Sherwood, "Tryout for Trivia." *Miami Herald*, March 22, 1985.

78 "and that pleased me to no end": "Alex Trebek Opens Up About Spirituality, Health." RAW/ABC7, September 17, 2019.

79 "even though we do well in a difficult job": Bettelou Peterson, "How Many Cosby Kids Are There?" *San Jose Mercury News*, June 16, 1985.

79 "Producing *Jeopardy!* for the last three years has whetted my appetite": Jerry Buck, "Master of the Games." *San Francisco Chronicle*, August 21, 1988.

79 "I don't want to be a game-show host forever": Dean Huber, "Game Show Hosts Bank Their Future on Wave of Popularity." *Sacramento Bee*, June 4, 1985.

81 "I don't have enough time to devote to a relationship": Ray Richmond, *This Is* Jeopardy!, Barnes & Noble Books, 2004.

81 "What his friends think is right for Alex is never what Alex thinks is right for Alex": Margot Dougherty, "Sorry, Girls, Mom Keeps House for *Jeopardy!* Host Alex Trebek." *People*, October 12, 1987.

82 "It's my weird sense of humor": Maralyn Lois Polak, "Interview." *Philadelphia Inquirer*, January 8, 1989.

82 "It's fine to care for animals, but show some concern for human suffering": Marla Brooks, "Alex Trebek Saves Cats in Jeopardy." *Cat Fancy*, January 2002.

82 "He's become so self-sufficient": Margot Dougherty, "Sorry, Girls, Mom Keeps House for *Jeopardy!* Host Alex Trebek." *People*, October 12, 1987.

83 "Flamingos and I have a great deal in common": Susan Schindehette, "Host of ABC's New *Super Jeopardy!*, Newlywed Alex Trebek Got the Answer Right with, 'Will You Marry Me?'" *People*, July 30, 1990.

84 "I felt it would work because it mixed products with talk": Martie Zad, "He's the Talented Host of *Jeopardy!*: Who Is Alex Trebek?" *Washington Post*, January 10, 1988.

84 "crap." Margot Dougherty, "Sorry, Girls, Mom Keeps House for *Jeopardy!* Host Alex Trebek." *People*, October 12, 1987.

84 "it behooves you to start giving back": Lisa LaFlamme, "Alex Trebek on His Health, Family, and Legacy." W5/CTV, October 5, 2019.

85 "I just looked at these children and thought, 'I've got to do something'": Ruta Lee, "Interview with Lee Meriwether and Alex Trebek." *Lifestyle Magazine*, November 29, 2012.

85 "I wanted to do something to help, more than just sending in a contribution": *The Charlie Rose Show*, November 16, 2006.

85 "It was heartbreaking stuff": Lisa LaFlamme, "Alex Trebek on His Health, Family, and Legacy." W5/CTV, October 5, 2019.

86 "We shouldn't have this problem in this rich country": Ruta Lee, "Interview with Lee Meriwether and Alex Trebek." *Lifestyle Magazine*, November 29, 2012.

6: SETTLING IN

87 "I'd become a terrible workaholic—[some days] you'd have to send me home in a Baggie": Martie Zad, "'Jeopardy' Host Is a Master Gamesman." *Washington Post*, January 11, 1988.

87 "I came home with two capes and a sword": Maralyn Lois Polak, "Interview." *Philadelphia Inquirer*, January 8, 1989.

88 "But I'd be replaced, and it's tough to get back in." Ibid.

88 "and so each day they added a few": Television Critics Association Winter Press Tour, January 8, 2020.

89 "People still ask me about that": Top Ten Things You Didn't Know About Alex Trebek, AskMen.com, September 26, 2010.

89 "Who are three people who've never been in my kitchen?": *Cheers*, "What Is . . . Cliff Clavin?" January 18, 1990.

89 "How can I go on hosting the program if I'm filled with all these doubts?" Ibid.

90 "if I ate forty of them that fortieth one would go down very

slowly": Susan Bickelhaupt, "Placing himself in *Jeopardy!* Tonight." *Boston Globe*, September 5, 1989.

90 "That's a little chintzy for me": Elizabeth Jensen, "Trivia Man with All The Answers." *Dallas Morning News*, November 10, 1990.

90 "You finish a dollar out of first place and you win a year's supply of lip gloss!": Franz Lidz, "What Is *Jeopardy!*?" *Sports Illustrated*, May 1, 1989.

90 "None of them seemed too concerned with grooming. I was very nervous about it": Ibid.

91 "people you'd see in a supermarket carefully pricing Campbell's Soup for One": Ibid.

91 "I'm [not] going to waste fifteen seconds by telling a joke": Patricia Ward Biederman, "On *Jeopardy!*, Timing Critical as Knowledge." *San Francisco Chronicle*, February 21, 1989.

92 "You're not the first woman to have said that, believe me!": Ray Richmond, *This Is* Jeopardy!, Barnes & Noble Books, 2004.

92 "she was most attractive and she thought I was a jerk": Harvey Levin, *OBJECTified*. Fox News, July 29, 2018.

92 "That's kind of spooky": Ruta Lee, "Interview with Lee Meriwether and Alex Trebek." *Lifestyle Magazine*, November 29, 2012.

93 "he's much more casual than he is on the show": Susan Schindehette, "Host of ABC's New *Super Jeopardy!*, Newlywed Alex Trebek Got the Answer Right with, 'Will You Marry Me?'" *People*, July 30, 1990.

93 "Having to focus on me is a challenge": Christina Gressianu, "Portrait Photography with Jean Trebek." YouTube, January 10, 2013.

93 "which I could confront any challenging situation": Jean Trebek, "Trusting in Myself." InsideWink.com, January 6, 2019.

94 "But it's nice to come home and let someone else do the nur-

turing": Harry Eisenberg, *Inside Jeopardy!*, Salt Lake City: North-west Publishing, 1993.

94 "There was just this deep sensitivity about him, with a gruffy exterior": Gillian Telling, "Inside Jeopardy! Host Alex Trebek's Sweet Love Story: 'I Just Wish I'd Met My Wife Earlier.'" *People*, January 24, 2019.

94 "Alex always had great taste, whether in music, books, crystal, or wives": Anne Gregor, "Jeopardy!'s Alex Trebek Gets Domestic." *Chatelaine*, December 1990.

94 "and he found her": Susan Schindehette, "Host of ABC's New *Super Jeopardy!*, Newlywed Alex Trebek Got the Answer Right with, 'Will You Marry Me?'" *People*, July 30, 1990.

94 "I feel terrible when we're apart": "Game Show Hosts," *The Phil Donahue Show*, 1988.

94 'The hell with it. We'll make it work": Susan Schindehette, "Host of ABC's New *Super Jeopardy!*, Newlywed Alex Trebek Got the Answer Right with, 'Will You Marry Me?'" *People*, July 30, 1990.

94 "We just took it one day at a time": Ibid.

95 "then don't ring in just yet": Alex Trebek, "How to Pop the Question." *Men's Health*, November 1998.

95 "Here's a little something else": Susan Schindehette, "Host of ABC's New *Super Jeopardy!*, Newlywed Alex Trebek Got the Answer Right with, 'Will You Marry Me?'" *People*, July 30, 1990.

95 "this is the first time I've said it out loud": "Morning Report." *Los Angeles Times*, September 15, 1989.

95 "We feel the same powerful kind of love Heathcliff and Cathy felt": Leah Garchik, "Personals." *San Francisco Chronicle*, May 5, 1993.

95 "That's the way Jeannie and I think of ourselves": *Turner Classic Movies Film Festival*, April 13, 2019.

96 "That's why I'm paid big bucks": Marian Christy, "Alex Trebek

Adjusts to Spending His Life in *Jeopardy!*" *Boston Globe*, November 7, 1990.

96 "but you can't let it bother you too much": Sarah Hampson, "And the Answer Is: Who Is Alex Trebek?" *Globe and Mail*, June 15, 2000.

97 "Is Alex here yet, and do you know his room number?" Felica Gressette, "Chocolate Conquers All." *Miami Herald*, March 10, 1994.

98 "My wife was upset, and my mother, a traditionalist, was angry": Marian Christy, "Alex Trebek Adjusts to Spending His Life in *Jeopardy!*" *Boston Globe*, November 7, 1990.

98 "But the situation took its toll on me": Ibid.

98 "The answer is . . . yes.": Susan Schindehette, "Host of ABC's *New Super Jeopardy!*, Newlywed Alex Trebek Got the Answer Right with, 'Will You Marry Me?' *People*, July 30, 1990.

99 "why people are the way they are and why they do the things they do": Ibid.

99 "They get along like a house on fire": Susan Schindehette, "Host of ABC's New *Super Jeopardy!*, Newlywed Alex Trebek Got the Answer Right with, 'Will You Marry Me?'" *People*, July 30, 1990.

99 "she's there for me in the evenings if Alex isn't home": Ibid.

99 "set in my ways": Alan Ebert, "We Visit with Alex Trebek." *Good Housekeeping*, August 1992.

99 'If you don't know what's expected, how can you do the right thing?": Marian Christy, "Alex Trebek Adjusts to Spending His Life in *Jeopardy!*" *Boston Globe*, November 7, 1990.

99 "it's best that each has a home to call her own": *Inside* Jeopardy! Harry Eisenberg, *Inside Jeopardy!*, Salt Lake City: Northwest Publishing, 1993.

100 "at a gut level—with this particular house": Alex Trebek Talk, Ukrainian Culture Center, Los Angeles, August 21, 2011.

101 "There is a power up there that influences us in ways we never know about": Ibid.

101 "I try to cope as best as I can with what's going on as it is happening": "Alex Trebek Opens Up About Spirituality, Health." RAW/ABC7, September 17, 2019.

101 "Doing that has allowed me to develop as a human": David Marchese, "In Conversation: Alex Trebek." *Vulture*, November 19, 2018.

101 "then there's something wrong with you": A. J. Jacobs, "What I've Learned." *Esquire*, April 2003.

7: FINDING FAMILY

102 "even though we may watch *The Gong Show* on a regular basis": QTV with Jian Ghomeshi, CBC, June 23, 2008.

103 "There's even a three-act structure." Jake Rossen, "A Brief History of *Jeopardy!*" *Mental Floss*, March 26, 2014.

103 "in order to achieve their fifteen minutes of fame": Dave McGinn, "We Asked Him 10 Questions. Who Is Alex Trebek?" *Globe and Mail*, June 11, 2013.

104 "'What does that person in the living room want to know right now?'": *Alex Trebek Talks CBC at 75*. CBC, November 2, 2011.

104 "as the impartial host I accept disorder": David Marchese, "In Conversation: Alex Trebek." *Vulture*, November 19, 2018.

104 "I have a way of looking at people that makes them feel uncomfortable": Maralyn Lois Polak, "Interview." *Philadelphia Inquirer*, January 8, 1989.

104 "This is not rocket science": David Marchese, "In Conversation: Alex Trebek." *Vulture*, November 19, 2018.

104 "Those games are tougher to host": Robert Channick, "Alex Trebek (and Mustache) Return for 31st Season as *Jeopardy!* Host." *Chicago Tribune*, September 16, 2014.

105 "marriage and having a family has brought into my life is fear": Lisa LaFlamme, "Alex Trebek on His Health, Family, and Legacy." W5/CTV, October 5, 2019.

105 "I was talking a hundred miles an hour": Barry Rogers, "Alex Trebek: Game Show Host Extraordinaire." *Living Well* magazine, June 25, 2014.

106 "When I'm an old man, some young stud might want my wife!": Marian Christy, "Alex Trebek Adjusts to Spending His Life in *Jeopardy!*" *Boston Globe*, November 7, 1990.

106 "My powers of concentration seem to be diminishing": Matt Roush, "Trebek Isn't Playing Games on *Jeopardy!*" *USA Today*, October 25, 1990.

106 "I realized that I was starting to lose it": Top Ten Things You Didn't Know About Alex Trebek, AskMen.com, September 26, 2010.

107 "a successful adult life is very important to me": Matt Roush, "Trebek Isn't Playing Games on *Jeopardy!*" *USA Today*, October 25, 1990.

107 "as long as he enjoys it": Alan Ebert, "We Visit with Alex Trebek." *Good Housekeeping*, August 1992.

107 "more to me than my own." Ibid.

108 "They just said, 'We'll talk about it later'": Blair Crawford, "Local Man's Brother: Who's Alex Trebek?" *Windsor Star*, April 26, 1991.

108 "there was something between us": Ibid.

108 "Boxers or briefs?": Jessica Messier, "Alli Ross to Represent WPI on *Jeopardy!* 2018 College Championship." Worcester Polytechnic Institute, wpi.edu, April 12, 2018.

109 "Sometimes I can't believe it myself": Ibid.

109 "Finding Michael has brought a peace to Mom's life that she didn't have before": Alan Braham Smith, "Alex Trebek's Family Secret." *National Enquirer*, 1991.

109 "How can we be an affluent people and have homeless people on the streets?": Marian Christy, "Alex Trebek Adjusts to Spending His Life in *Jeopardy!*" *Boston Globe*, November 7, 1990.

110 "I like the way their furry coats wave in the breeze when they are running": "This Is Alex Trebek's Spirit Animal." Jeopardy .com, July 1, 2015.

112 "I taste the wines, but not in the sense of holding veto power over the experts": Paul Gilette, "Who is Alex Trebek?" *Wine Enthusiast*, February 1994.

113 "I fell in love with the property": "A CTV Portrait of Alex Trebek." CTV Television, December 7, 1996.

113 "I feel a little bit like Scarlett O'Hara's father": Ibid.

113 "didn't compare to watching your own horse run in the Kentucky Derby": Tim Price, "Equine Entry Fit for TV Host." *Fort Worth Star-Telegram*, April 27, 2002.

114 "It's like getting back to nature": Bob Mieszerski, "An Owner with the Answers." *Los Angeles Times*, June 13, 2003.

114 "but it's not a great house for toddlers": Ruth Ryon, "*Jeopardy!* Host Sells Bachelor Pad." *San Francisco Chronicle*, December 20, 1995.

114 "Alex comes over in work clothes and a *Jeopardy!* cap to fix it himself": Scott Raab, "The Hit King: Pete Rose in Purgatory." *Deadspin*, August 8, 2013.

115 "This house changes that": Alan Ebert, "We Visit with Alex Trebek." *Good Housekeeping*, August 1992.

8: BEHIND THE SCENES

117 "If you know the correct response all the time, you're not as involved": Chris Hardwick, "Alex Trebek." *Nerdist*, May 16, 2014.

117 "and I don't want to come off like a schmuck": *The Howard Stern Show*, May 11, 2015.

118 "it is one that the audience perceives requires maturity": Lee Alan Hill, "Trebek's Appeal Endures." *Television Week*, February 9, 2004.

118 "I don't blog, I don't tweet": Daniel Stone, "Is Alex Trebek in Jeopardy?" *Newsweek*, February 21, 2011.

119 "I may stumble on a fact": Kaitlin Provencher, "The Best Job for a Trivia-Loving English Major." *Tufts Now*, September 19, 2011.

119 "and suddenly you have four clues": "Alex Trebek, " *Rockburn Presents*. CPAC, July 11, 2013.

119 "that will help you get to the correct response": Michael O'Connell, "This . . . Is . . . the Man Who Runs *Jeopardy!*" *Hollywood Reporter*, April 26, 2017.

119 "MILLARD FILLMORE 'SHUFFLED OFF' THE PROVERBIAL MORTAL COIL IN THIS CITY": Ken Jennings, "Interview with Carlo Panno, Continued." Ken-Jennings .com, March 28, 2008.

120 "'Gee, I *should* have known that'": David Friedman, "*Jeopardy!* Writers Know All the Answers." *Dallas Morning News*, March 22, 1987.

120 "The capital of Romania, for example—who cares what it is?": Ibid.

120 "I can say, 'This is too tough and nobody will get it'": Barrie Nedler, Interview. Television Academy Foundation, August 22, 2007.

120–121 "Damn, you guys gave me some really tough stuff today": Ibid.

121 "We essentially try to confirm that the first source was right": "What It Takes to Be a *Jeopardy!* Researcher." *JBuzz Blog*, July 10, 2018.

121 "To me, Alex looks best in a rich, dark suit": Rosemary Counter, "Meet the Man Who Dresses Alex Trebek." *Vanity Fair*, January 6, 2016.

122 "he needs to be in green": Ibid.

122 "His weight and measurements stayed exactly the same": Ray Richmond, *This Is* Jeopardy!, Barnes & Noble Books, 2004.

122 "I really enjoy talking to the audiences": Noreen Malone, "The Last King of the American Middlebrow." *New Republic*, May 26, 2014.

123 "so I joke with them and they love it": Barrie Nedler, Interview. Television Academy Foundation, August 22, 2007.

124 "like a hummingbird having a seizure": Amanda Mannen, "6 Inside Facts About Jeopardy from a 74-Episode Winner." Cracked.com, April 21, 2015.

124 "writing with an icicle on glass": Ibid.

125 "I do want to keep it light because it is a fairly serious show": Barrie Nedler, Interview. Television Academy Foundation, August 22, 2007.

125 "'Do you plan to throw axes again in competition?'": Larry Keller and Christian Millman, and the Editors of *Men's Health* Books, *Guy Knowledge*. Emmaus, Pennsylvania: Rodale Press, Inc. 1999.

126 "you don't know what the category is about": "Who is Alex Trebek? Celebrating 35 Seasons of *Jeopardy!*" 92Y Talk with Michael McKean, February 19, 2019.

126 "if you know the correct response to everything that's up there": *The Howard Stern Show*, May 11, 2015.

126 "I'm worried about your language": Alex Trebek, *The Dan Patrick Show*, August 8, 2014.

126 "I was not having a good time.": Jessica Messier, "Alli Ross to Represent WPI on *Jeopardy!* 2018 College Championship." Worcester Polytechnic Institute, wpi.edu, April 12, 2018.

127 "Good players are usually well-read and interested in a wide variety of things": Nicole Brodeur, "*Jeopardy!* Auditions." *Seattle Times*, July 27, 2017.

127 "You could be the *host* of the show, but not a contestant": "A CTV Portrait of Alex Trebek." CTV Television, December 7, 1996.

127 "How could you make that absurd Daily Double wager?": Alex McLevy, "What's It Like to Be One of the *Jeopardy!* Clue Writers?" AV Club, March 12, 2015.

128 "I have borrowed new ways of doing that from the others": Lee Alan Hill, "Trebek's Appeal Endures." *Television Week*, February 9, 2004.

128 "we think that has helped us appeal to a broader audience": Paige Albiniak, "What Is Categorically Just as Dynamic at 30?" *Broadcasting & Cable*, March 31, 2014.

129 "who is the voice of the character Homer on *The Simpsons*": Ibid.

129 "It's sad, but there's not much anyone can do": Noreen Malone, "The Last King of the American Middlebrow." *New Republic*, May 26, 2014.

129 "I need other people to come up to me and tell me": "Alex Trebek." Success Talk with Peter Lowe, 1997.

130 "and I liked him a lot": Ken Jennings, "Interview with Carlo Panno, Concluded." Ken-Jennings.com, March 31, 2008.

130 "What kind of crap is that?": Barrie Nedler, Interview. Television Academy Foundation, August 22, 2007.

130 "You start and you go on forever": Graham Flanagan, "We Spent a Day Behind the Scenes of *Jeopardy!* with Alex Trebek." *Business Insider*, April 5, 2019.

9: BRANCHING OUT

132 "but do it in a positive way, and not that he should do *anything* to win": "Alex Trebek." Success Talk with Peter Lowe, 1997.

133 "No one wants to go out and look bad": Gina Shaffer, "The Category Is Celebrities Playing *Jeopardy!* This Week." *Fort Worth Star-Telegram*, October 27, 1992.

134 "there's nothing we can do": "People." *Contra Costa Times*, November 9, 1996.

134 "all of a sudden they're on their own having to face tough questions": "Who is Alex Trebek? Celebrating 35 Seasons of *Jeopardy!*" 92Y Talk with Michael McKean, February 19, 2019.

134 "I'm [afraid I'll] choke and embarrass myself": Jonah Engel Bromwich, "Why America Loves Alex Trebek." *New York Times*, March 8, 2019.

134 "'Oh, he's being a smart-ass' and won't want me anymore": Alex Trebek, *The Dan Patrick Show*, August 8, 2014.

135 "He was bright, very knowledgeable and he won his game": Alex Trebek, *Live with Kelly and Ryan*, February 21, 2019.

135 "the prospect of appearing on national television and embarrassing themselves": Robert Channick, "Alex Trebek (and Mustache) Return for 31st Season as *Jeopardy!* Host." *Chicago Tribune*, September 16, 2014.

135 "your audience will immediately recognize who you're poking fun at": Alex Trebek, *The Dan Patrick Show*, August 8, 2014.

135 "He looked more the part too, with the dark hair and mustache": Ibid.

137 "And he seemed to be enjoying himself": "The Maestro." *People*, November 21, 1994.

138 "I'm comfortable being myself, but it got to be tiresome for me": Barrie Nedler, Interview. Television Academy Foundation, August 22, 2007.

138 "people probably think I can do that anyway": Ericka Souter, "Chatter." *People*, May 6, 2002.

138 "because he had touched [star] David Duchovny": Top Ten Things You Didn't Know About Alex Trebek, AskMen.com, September 26, 2010.

139 "all of the things that they're going to throw at me": Chris Hardwick, "Alex Trebek." *Nerdist*, May 16, 2014.

140 "I'm still having a lot of fun doing what I'm doing": Gary Dretzka and Robert Edelstein, "He Gives Answers for a Change." *Broadcasting & Cable*, February 12, 2007.

140 "so there's no need to do it": Barry Rogers, "Alex Trebek: Game Show Host Extraordinaire." *Living Well Magazine*, June 25, 2014.

140 "and it isn't going to work here": Jan Wong, *Lunch with Jan Wong*. Doubleday Canada, 2000. February 6, 1997.

141 "You're going to a different world—emotionally, spiritually, and physically": Fast Talk: Alex Trebek." *Travel + Leisure*, May 29, 2009.

141 "you're not a good traveler at all": Brittany Chrusciel, "What's on Alex Trebek's Bucket List (and Why He Thinks You're Not a Good Traveler)." SmarterTravel.com, June 19, 2017.

141 "People marvel at our packing skills": Fast Talk: Alex Trebek." *Travel + Leisure*, May 29, 2009.

142 "and that makes me feel really good": *Alex Trebek Talks CBC at 75*. CBC, November 2, 2011.

142 "I see no black people on it": "Talking with David Frost: Maya Angelou." PBS, 1995.

142 "It could be that they're afraid of embarrassing themselves": *The Howard Stern Show*, May 11, 2015.

143 "more aware of the accomplishments of black people in this country": Chuck Taylor, "'Jeopardy' Host Defends Show's Record on Race." *Seattle Times*, November 2, 1995.

143 "'Let's get together and get along'": *The Howard Stern Show*, May 11, 2015.

143 "men act like it's not real money until the end of the show": Gillian Telling, "Alex Trebek: What I Know Now." *People*, February 4, 2019.

143 "blaming it on the woman instead of saying that the show wasn't very good": "Alex Trebek." Success Talk with Peter Lowe, 1997.

144 "but where are they when we're not fighting?": Barrie Nedler, Interview. Television Academy Foundation, August 22, 2007.

145 "that's a geographic event": Gloria Galloway. "What Makes Alex Trebek a Man of the World?" *Globe and Mail*, November 5, 2010.

145 "It covers everything, really": Harry Wilson, "Alex Trebek." *Canadian Geographic*, April 2015.

146 "I've always liked low-fat milk": Graham Flanagan, "We Spent a Day Behind the Scenes of *Jeopardy!* with Alex Trebek." *Business Insider*, April 5, 2019.

146 "You have to wonder about some of the contestants on that show": Bill Hoffman, "Trebek: *Millionaire* Wins No Prizes." *New York Post*, March 20, 2000.

147 "we'll see if you can remember what color Post-its are!": Ibid.

147 "I'll tell her to stop reading my mind, but she'll say that she thought of it, too": Ruta Lee, "Interview with Lee Meriwether and Alex Trebek." *Lifestyle Magazine*, November 29, 2012.

147 "I don't care if I never go out in Hollywood": Knowlton Nash, *Cue the Elephant*. Toronto: McClelland & Stewart, 1996.

10: SHIFTING GEARS

149 "They brought us in to give the show a new look": Daniel Stone, "Is Alex Trebek in Jeopardy?" *Newsweek*, February 21, 2011.

149 "Jean asked how taping went that day": Barrie Nedler, Interview. Television Academy Foundation, August 22, 2007.

150 "Oh my God, you shaved your mustache": Ibid.

150 "and they're asking about my mustache": Ibid.

150 "But I got to enjoy the wine, at least": Chris Taylor, "*Jeopardy!*

Host Alex Trebek Provides a Few Answers of His Own." Reuters, March 23, 2017.

150 "to ease the blow for them": Jeanne Wolf, "Three Questions: Alex Trebek." *Saturday Evening Post*, January/February 2016.

151 "in the minds of some people, a little snobby?": Ben Reiter, "CATCHING UP WITH . . . *Jeopardy!*" *Sports Illustrated*, May 4, 2009.

151 "I can't show favoritism": "An Audio Daily Double." *Newsweek*, May 20, 2002.

151 "we were entertained by the most glorious oak trees, deer, and birds of all sorts": Jean Trebek, "Letting Go." InsideWink .com, September 3, 2019.

152 "and in being wise to the sensitivities of my home": Lisa LaFlamme, "A Conversation with Alex Trebek." CBC, December 18, 2019.

152 "because you could do it faster": Emily Gawlek, "How *Jeopardy!* Host Alex Trebek Stays Mentally Sharp and Physically Fit." *Media Planet/USA Today*, December 28, 2018.

152 "They will abandon me at the weirdest moments": Graham Flanagan, "We Spent a Day Behind the Scenes of *Jeopardy!* with Alex Trebek." *Business Insider*, April 5, 2019.

153 "You never see that beam above you!": Frazier Moore, "Alex Trebek: Longtime Host of *Jeopardy!* Still Has All the Answers." *Alaska Highway News*, June 4, 2012.

153 "I'm not likely to get on the treadmill": Graham Flanagan, "We Spent a Day Behind the Scenes of *Jeopardy!* with Alex Trebek." *Business Insider*, April 5, 2019.

153 "if I'm doing physical labor I never think of food [or water]": Alex Ben Block and Philiana Ng, "Alex Trebek on *Jeopardy!*'s Longevity, His Health Issues and When He Might Retire." *Hollywood Reporter*, May 14, 2014.

154 "lightning-fast finger and computer-file memory": Rick Kushman, "The Big Winner on *Jeopardy!* Is Like a Robot." *Sacramento Bee*, June 28, 2004.

155 "he understood the nuances, knew how to wager, and was funny": Barrie Nedler, Interview. Television Academy Foundation, August 22, 2007.

155 "It became the Ken and Alex Show": Timothy Gunatilaka, "DVD Q&A: ALEX TREBEK." *Entertainment Weekly*, November 18, 2005.

155 "I was spending more time with Ken Jennings than I was with my wife": "10 Questions." *Time*, September 14, 2009.

155 "I couldn't think of any questions to ask him anymore": Barrie Nedler, Interview. Television Academy Foundation, August 22, 2007.

156 "Anything with a mullet . . . and I was done": Lauren Ready, "Ken Jennings: Greatest 'Jeopardy!' Champ Tells All." *USA Today*, November 20, 2013.

156 "I couldn't find my groove": Tom Gliatto, "What Is $2,520,700?" *People*, December 13, 2004.

157 "My first thought was, 'But Ken doesn't lose'": Ibid.

157 "I very much doubt that we will ever see an accomplishment like this again": Press release, *JEOPARDY!* Streak Over. King World Productions, November 30, 2004.

157 "Ken's gone. My buddy, my pal": Barrie Nedler, Interview. Television Academy Foundation, August 22, 2007.

157 "so I could see every pore of Alex Trebek": Lauren Ready, "Ken Jennings: Greatest *Jeopardy!* Champ Tells All." *USA Today*, November 20, 2013.

158 "how some of the past *Jeopardy!* players would do against him": Associated Press, December 29, 2004.

159 "'What am I going to do today?'": "Fun Keeps Alex Trebek Playing *Jeopardy!*" Associated Press, June 6, 2007.

159 "I read that script, and I had tears in my eyes": "Who is Alex Trebek? Celebrating 35 Seasons of *Jeopardy!*" 92Y Talk with Michael McKean, February 19, 2019.

159–160 "[Dad] would be fine eating chicken, white rice, and broccoli for the rest of his life": "Matt Trebek: Bringing Mexican Street Food to Harlem." *Fordham News*, October 27, 2016.

160 "We all knew Dad would be out five seconds later fixing it": "A Father's Day Story from Emily Trebek." Jeopardy.com, June 14, 2017.

160 "It's truly an honor to be recognized by your own country": Bruce Demara, "Our Walk with Fame." *Toronto Star*, June 4, 2006.

161 "the show is better for it": Devon Ivie, "*Jeopardy!*'s Ken Jennings Tells Us His 'Perfect' Alex Trebek Story." *Vulture*, March 7, 2019.

161 "I have regretted it afterwards": QTV with Jian Ghomeshi, CBC, June 23, 2008.

162 "there was a high rate of cancer among people in the area, including their relatives": "*Jeopardy!* Host Alex Trebek & Family Doomed by Cancer Curse." RadarOnline.com, October 3, 2019.

162 "like when a mother sings a lullaby to her baby": Caroline Hopkins, "Jean Trebek Tells SurvivorNet 'The Universe Will Always Respond' When You Ask for Help." Survivornet.com, November 20, 2019.

163 "I'm willing to try everything once": Leah Binkovitz, "Alex Trebek on Why *Jeopardy!* Represents the American Dream." Smithsonian.com, May 9, 2013.

163 "Then again, I don't pass too many people on the freeway either": Dennis Dean, "Grand Prix: Alex Trebek Won't Jeopardize Safety Next Week." *Long Beach Post*, April 8, 2009.

11: GIVING BACK

164 "if there are groups in need, we try to help them": Chris Taylor, "*Jeopardy!* Host Alex Trebek Provides a Few Answers of His Own." Reuters, March 23, 2017.

164 "and never expecting anything in return": Laura Eggertson, "Alex Trebek Gift Supports Big Thinking." University of Ottawa, May 4, 2016.

164 "but you have to make a few decisions": Chris Hardwick, "Alex Trebek." *Nerdist*, May 16, 2014.

165 "and have done their due diligence in their respective endeavors": Lisa LaFlamme, "Alex Trebek on His Health, Family, and Legacy." W5/CTV, October 5, 2019.

165 "They're really the best of Alex and me": Gillian Telling, "Inside *Jeopardy!* Host Alex Trebek's Sweet Love Story: 'I Just Wish I'd Met My Wife Earlier.'" *People*, January 24, 2019.

165 "it helps many other deserving students have that same transformational experience": Bob Howe, "This Tremendously Popular Quiz Show Host Has Endowed a $1 Million Scholarship at Fordham." *Fordham News*, October 8, 2015.

166 "It gives me a great deal of joy": Chris Hardwick, "Alex Trebek." *Nerdist*, May 16, 2014.

166 "the same dirty water hole where cattle were drinking": Melanie Grayce West, "Donor of the Day: *Jeopardy!* Host Funds Fordham." *Wall Street Journal*, October 7, 2015.

166 "So the smaller the area of help, the better it is": Ibid.

167 "so I guess you did the best [you could] for your species": Daniel Stone, "Is Alex Trebek in Jeopardy?" *Newsweek*, February 21, 2011.

168 "As far as taking a dislike to a particular contestant, [it was] only Watson": "Who Is Alex Trebek? Celebrating 35 Seasons of *Jeopardy!*" 92Y Talk with Michael McKean, February 19, 2019.

168 "I guess that's not too far off": Daniel Stone, "Is Alex Trebek in Jeopardy?" *Newsweek*, February 21, 2011.

168 "fell in an ignominious heap to the carpeting": Tony Hicks, "People." *Contra Costa Times*, July 28, 2011.

169 "So I now have two": "Who Is Alex Trebek? Celebrating 35 Seasons of *Jeopardy!*" 92Y Talk with Michael McKean, February 19, 2019.

169 "it's been in the San Francisco dump [ever since]": Ibid.

170 "so I'm used to dealing with pain": "Alex Trebek on his Fight Against Cancer." The National Interview, CBC News, May 13, 2019.

170 "I wouldn't count on it": Patrick Gomez, "Alex Trebek: My Heart Attack Had My Wife in Tears with Worry." *People*, June 28, 2012.

170 "If I thought [exercise] was really important, I would do it": Julie Mazziotta, "Inside Alex Trebek's Health Battles Throughout His 35 Years on *Jeopardy!*" *People*, March 6, 2019.

171 "Saying that I've *thought* about retiring doesn't mean that I'm *doing* it": Frazier Moore, "*Jeopardy!* Host Alex Trebek Has All the Answers." Associated Press, May 29, 2012.

171 "[Thirty] has a nice ring to it": *FOX News Sunday with Chris Wallace*, *News Sunday with Chris Wallace*, Fox News, May 6, 2012.

171 "I'm getting on her nerves because I'm around all the time": Gillian Telling and Christina Dugan, "Alex Trebek Said He'd 'Be Lost' Without *Jeopardy!* 2 Months Before Cancer Diagnosis." *People*, March 6, 2019.

171 "She was upset about not being able to completely play the game to the end": "What Is . . . a Hissy Fit?" *Radar Online*, December 16, 2014.

172 "If I'm making mistakes and saying things you don't like, maybe it's time for me to move on": Ibid.

172 "they don't know how to fail": David Marchese, "In Conversation: Alex Trebek." *Vulture*, November 19, 2018.

172 "I feel for them": Melody Kramer, "Alex Trebek: On Hosting the National Geographic Bee." *National Geographic*, May 21, 2013.

172 "It frightens me that we're losing sensitivity toward others": Gillian Telling, "Alex Trebek: What I Know Now." *People*, February 4, 2019.

173 "to take the time to sit down and write a letter": Chris Hardwick, "Alex Trebek." *Nerdist*, May 16, 2014.

173 "Why is it important to know what I did this morning and convey that to other people?": Ibid.

174 "The lack of continuity makes it feel weird to say it's the fiftieth anniversary": Ben Cosman, "Why Doesn't 'Jeopardy!' Care About Its 50th Birthday?" *The Wire*, March 27, 2014.

174 "that's what defines his appeal": Robert Edelstein, "Alex Trebek." *Broadcasting & Cable*, October 28, 2013.

175 "We try to get some things that sound a little bit goofy coming out of Alex's mouth": Brian Josephs, "*Jeopardy!* Head Writer Billy Wisse on Those Viral Music Questions and Making Alex Trebek Rap." *Spin*, March 10, 2017.

175 "Traveling more would be nice": Daniel Stone, "Is Alex Trebek in Jeopardy?" *Newsweek*, February 21, 2011.

176 "in a very short time he or she would win them over": Dave McGinn, "We Asked Him 10 Questions. Who Is Alex Trebek?" *Globe and Mail*, June 11, 2013.

176 "There is a time for all things, and my time might be coming": William Keck, "Keck's Exclusives: Alex Trebek on Retiring from *Jeopardy* and His Possible Successor." *TV Guide*, May 9, 2013.

12: LETTING GO

177 "I'm not ultraconservative, but I'm not ultraliberal either": David Marchese, "In Conversation: Alex Trebek." *Vulture*, November 19, 2018.

178 "not somebody whose negativity will take us all down": Andrew Dunn, "Alex Trebek: 2016 Race 'Disappointing on Both Sides.'" TheHill.com, April 11, 2016.

178 "Who'd want to do that?": James Bradshaw, "Trebek Defends *Jeopardy!* on the CBC." *Globe and Mail*, March 17, 2009.

178 "it's all we do every day": David Marchese, "In Conversation: Alex Trebek." *Vulture*, November 19, 2018.

178 "make people feel good about themselves, their accomplishments, and the country": "Who Is Alex Trebek? Celebrating 35 Seasons of *Jeopardy!*" 92Y Talk with Michael McKean, February 19, 2019.

178 "it's because it wasn't all that important to me": Noreen Malone, "The Last King of the American Middlebrow." *New Republic*, May 26, 2014.

178 "'There are scientists who don't agree'": David Marchese, "In Conversation: Alex Trebek." *Vulture*, November 19, 2018.

178 "Those of you who do not believe in global warming, shut up": Valerie Block, "Trebek: Climate in Jeopardy." *Crain's New York Business*, October 28, 2013.

179 "It scared the daylights out of me": "Alex Trebek on his Fight Against Cancer." The National Interview, CBC News, May 13, 2019.

180 "When it's clear that it's time for me to go, I'll go": David Marchese, "In Conversation: Alex Trebek." *Vulture*, November 19, 2018.

180 "I don't have the kind of ego that would drive me to be wheeled onstage": Gary Dretzka and Robert Edelstein, "He Gives Answers for a Change." *Broadcasting & Cable*, February 12, 2007.

180 "things got a little out of hand—hairs kept attracting friends": *Jeopardy!*, September 10, 2011.

181 "What is chunky, yet funky?": RuPaul on *Jeopardy!* April 23, 2018.

182 "What on earth was I thinking?": Antonia Noori Farzan, "Alex Trebek Moderated a Gubernatorial Debate in Pennsylvania. It Didn't Go Well." *Washington Post*, October 2, 2018.

182 "is pretty remarkable for a thirty-five-year-old show": Danielle Turchiano, "All-Star Anniversary Competition." *Variety*, February 27, 2019.

182 "or my grandmother used to watch'": Ibid.

182 "a bulge in his stomach the size of a small fist": "*Jeopardy!* Host Alex Trebek on his Cancer Diagnosis." *CBS Sunday Morning*, May 12, 2019.

183 "I wanted our viewers to get the facts straight from the horse's mouth": "Alex Trebek Opens Up About Spirituality, Health." RAW/ABC7, September 17, 2019.

183 "this week I was diagnosed with stage 4 pancreatic cancer": "A Message from Alex Trebek." *Jeopardy!* YouTube channel, March 6, 2019.

184 "It was like the Grand Canyon getting leukemia": Sam Anderson, "Blue Yonder." *New York Times Magazine*, December 8, 2019.

184 "For him to express a kind of vulnerability has really touched a lot of people": "What Is *Jeopardy!?*" *ABC News Special with Michael Strahan*, January 2, 2020.

184 "I seemed a little slower in the ad-lib portions": Television Critics Association Winter Press Tour, January 8, 2020.

184 "We're doing the shows": "*Jeopardy!* Host Alex Trebek on his Cancer Diagnosis." *CBS Sunday Morning*, May 12, 2019.

185 "I can always suck it up when it comes time to tape the show": Lisa LaFlamme, "Alex Trebek on His Health, Family, and Legacy." W5/CTV, October 5, 2019.

185 "and also a lot of cannabis from well-wishers": "Alex Trebek Thanks His Supporters: 'We Will Meet Again.'" Royal Canadian Geographical Society, May 13, 2019.

186 "learning at least the basics of every subject I could imagine popping up on the show": Emma Lombardozzi, "*Jeopardy!* Champion Holzhauer Fulfilling a Life-long Promise." *Sams Salmon Exclusive*, May 2, 2019.

186 "There are moments in the games when I'm thinking, 'How the hell did he know that?'": "*Jeopardy!* Host Alex Trebek on his Cancer Diagnosis." *CBS Sunday Morning*, May 12, 2019.

187 "James's performance, I'm sure, is causing grief for an accountant somewhere": Joe Pinsker, "*Jeopardy!* Wasn't Designed for a Contestant Like James Holzhauer." *The Atlantic*, April 20, 2019.

187 "who have expressed their good thoughts, their positive energy, and their prayers": Gillian Telling and Christina Dugan, "Never Giving Up Hope: Alex Trebek." *People*, June 10, 2019.

187 "I've discovered that I'm a bit of a wuss, but I'm fighting through it": *Good Morning America*, May 1, 2019.

187 "Let me tell you, it's going to be a good year": Jeopardy .com, August 29, 2019.

188 "The immunotherapy didn't do diddly-squat": Lisa La-Flamme, "Alex Trebek on His Health, Family, and Legacy." W5/ CTV, October 5, 2019.

188 "I leave home and I'm in terrible shape sometimes": Gary Levin, "Alex Trebek on Pancreatic Cancer Battle." *USA Today*, November 20, 2019.

188 "And the pain moves": Alex Coleman, "Alex Trebek Talks to WREG about Hosting *Jeopardy!* After Cancer Diagnosis." WREG-TV, February 13, 2020.

188 "The adrenaline kicks in and I go out onstage and it seems to work": Gary Levin, "Alex Trebek on Pancreatic Cancer Battle." *USA Today*, November 20, 2019.

188 "which makes it difficult for me to speak and enunciate properly": Lisa LaFlamme, "Alex Trebek on His Health, Family, and Legacy." W5/CTV, October 5, 2019.

189 "because I don't communicate that much": "Alex Trebek Opens Up About Spirituality, Health." RAW/ABC7, September 17, 2019.

189 "I'm not always the most pleasant person to be around when I'm experiencing severe pain or depression": "What Is *Jeopardy!*?" *ABC News Special with Michael Strahan*, January 2, 2020.

189 "in pain and I can't help him": Ibid.

190 "It bothers me that I might pass on before I get to have a grandchild": Lisa LaFlamme, "Alex Trebek on His Health, Family, and Legacy." W5/CTV, October 5, 2019.

190 "Why wouldn't I want to continue to do this as long as I can?": "Alex Trebek Opens Up About Spirituality, Health." RAW/ABC7, September 17, 2019.

190 "He has his own family over there; they're such a close-knit, beautiful group of people": "What Is *Jeopardy!*?" *ABC News Special with Michael Strahan*, January 2, 2020.

190 "'Bittersweet' is the perfect word to describe the feeling I have about the sale of our home": Jean Trebek, "Letting Go." InsideWink.com, September 3, 2019.

191 "We were all hurting for him so badly": @dhruvg_, Twitter, November 12, 2019.

191 "but really, I just kept thinking about Alex": Ibid.

191 "That's very kind of you; thank you": *Jeopardy!*, November 11, 2019.

192 "what everybody at the tournament was thinking." @dhruvg_, Twitter, November 12, 2019.

192 "because there's a little too much of Alex Trebek out there right now": Lisa LaFlamme, "Alex Trebek on His Health, Family, and Legacy." W5/CTV, October 5, 2019.

192 "it does place a responsibility on me that I feel I'm not deserving of": Ibid.

192 "so it's tough on me": Ibid.

193 "But I'm not scared to death, so maybe I am courageous": "What Is *Jeopardy!*?" *ABC News Special with Michael Strahan*, January 2, 2020.

193 "I'm not gonna delude myself": Lisa LaFlamme, "Alex Trebek on His Health, Family, and Legacy." W5/CTV, October 5, 2019.

193 "such an impact on the lives of so many people out there": "Channel 11's Jennifer Tomazic Sits Down with *Jeopardy!* Host Alex Trebek." WPXI-TV, February 10, 2020.

193 "But *I* get to see it": Jacob Uitti, "Ken Jennings Talks Strategy, Marvel Movies, and Alex Trebek." Interview.com, February 10, 2020.

193 "He's got it under control, and we need that": Devon Ivie, "*Jeopardy!*'s Ken Jennings Tells Us His 'Perfect' Alex Trebek Story." *Vulture*, March 7, 2019.

194 "and it doesn't bother me in the least": Dan Zak, "Alex Trebek, Thinking Deep After 28 Seasons of *Jeopardy!*" *Washington Post*, April 29, 2012.

194 "'He was taken from us too soon'": Lisa LaFlamme, "Alex Trebek on His Health, Family, and Legacy." W5/CTV, October 5, 2019.

194 "l learned it from the Jesuits when I was a kid": Christopher White, "Alex Trebek Award by Fordham University 'Not Just About Trivia.'" *Crux*, January 14, 2020.

194 "There are so many talented people out there that could do the job": "Who is Alex Trebek? Celebrating 35 Seasons of *Jeopardy!*" 92Y Talk with Michael McKean, February 19, 2019.

194 "I'm not emotionally prepared for that": Jacob Uitti, "Ken Jennings Talks Strategy, Marvel Movies, and Alex Trebek." Interview.com, February 10, 2020.

195 "God bless you and goodbye": Television Critics Association Winter Press Tour January 8, 2020.

INDEX

Ben Gately Williams

LISA ROGAK is the author of numerous books, including *Rachel Maddow: A Biography*, *And Nothing But the Truthiness: The Rise (and Further Rise) of Stephen Colbert*, and the *New York Times* bestseller *Angry Optimist: The Life and Times of Jon Stewart*. She is the editor of the *New York Times* bestseller *Barack Obama in His Own Words*. Rogak lives in New Hampshire. Learn more at www.lisarogak.com.